Members Only?
Parliament in the Public Eye

The Report of the
Hansard Society Commission
on the Communication of
Parliamentary Democracy

HANSARD
SOCIETY

Hansard Society, 9 Kingsway, London WC2B 6XF

Published on behalf of the Hansard Society by Dod's Parliamentary Communications, Westminster Tower, 3 Albert Embankment, London SE1 7SP.

ISBN 0 900432 77 2

Typesetting by Dod's Parliamentary Communications
Printed in Great Britain by Unwin Brothers, The Gresham Press, Old Woking, Surrey

Members of the Commission

Acknowledgements
This report was drafted by Yusef Azad, Consultant to the Commission, and Gemma Rosenblatt, Managing Clerk. The Commission is grateful for the invaluable support and advice it received from the Hansard Society. In particular, the Commission would like to thank Alex Brazier, Virginia Gibbons, sub-editor to the report, Clare Ettinghausen and Angelo Evangelou. The Commission was supported by the research work of Shannon Granville and Ragnhild Handagard and appreciates the assistance of Jennifer Roberts and Vanessa Scott.

The Commission is grateful to the wide range of individuals and organisations who contributed to our inquiry and for the assistance we received from a number of parliamentary clerks and officials. Our findings were complemented by the work of Kierra Box, Joe Hall, Christina Jessah and Roz Mascarenhas, who together formed our Young People's Working Group, as organised by the Carnegie Young People Initiative. The Commission would also like to thank Paula Carter for her continuous and informed support.

Finally, the Commission could not have proceeded without the support of our sponsors: BBC, Ofcom, ITC and Channel 4 at the outset; and we are also grateful to Clear Channel International and Johnston Press.

Contents

Preface

Over the years the Hansard Society has initiated a number of high-level Commissions to deliberate and report on major issues of public policy, as they relate, in the main, in Parliament. Our Reports have always had a useful impact on informed opinion and have, on a number of occasions, also led to changes in policy or practice.

This Report, *Members Only? Parliament in the Public Eye*, is particularly important and indeed timely. We have just emerged from an election which generated more heat than light; and it would be difficult to maintain that it has left the profession of politics in high repute. No-one at Westminster can ignore the evidence of widespread cynicism and voter alienation, which is in danger of lapping at the skirts of the Mother of Parliaments herself.

Yet this is not to say that British citizens are uninterested in the issues of the day. Quite the reverse. It is more that they see a weak connection between their concerns and their perceptions of how Parliament works and what it does.

It is an enormous strength of this Report, for which I thank Lord Puttnam and his colleagues on the Commission, that they do not fall into the easy trap of blaming the messenger, the media in this case, for the lack of enthusiasm and respect for the work of Parliament. It is too easy for Parliamentarians, of whom there were distinguished representatives on the Commission, to rail at the media with the same fury which Caliban vented upon the glass in which he saw himself.

The Commission has been forthright in recommending ways, some obvious and overdue and some more visionary and perhaps provocative to traditionalists, in which Parliament could remove the beam from its own eye.

Equally, despite the participation of leading journalists on the Commission, there has been no reticence in addressing motes in the eye of the media which distort and diminish people's understanding of their legislature.

The Hansard Society in thanking Lord Puttnam's Commission for an outstanding Report, and those benign sponsors who made it possible, pledges itself to secure the widest possible debate of their conclusions in the hope that, as so often before, we can successfully change the parliamentary weather for the good.

Richard Holme
Rt Hon Lord Holme of Cheltenham CBE
Chair, Hansard Society

Foreword

'We the people' is surely the most succinct declaration of democratic intent ever drafted in the English language – with 'Government of the People by the People for the People' running a pretty close second. We in Britain have nothing similar, clearly there were no would-be Thomas Jeffersons sitting among the Barons when the Magna Carta was written! However, in the weeks running up to the May 2005 General Election the people of this country could well have believed that the practices of their own Parliament were soundly based on 'Jeffersonian' principles.

On the face of it, their opinions were sought, studied, taken account of, adjusted for, and whenever possible manipulated in support of this or that party or policy. And it's likely to happen again in four or five years – but not all that often in between. Modern technology may have provided the means for a more fully informed electorate, but Parliament itself has yet to summon up the will.

If we the people really are as important as we were encouraged to believe, then this Report is a timely reminder to Parliament of the enormous amount that remains to be done in closing the communication gap between itself and the electorate.

When more than two-thirds of first-time voters choose not to use their franchise, when the vote of only one person in 20 is considered significant in determining the outcome of a General Election, and when <u>any</u> Government can achieve power with the support of less than 25 per cent of those eligible to vote, it can only be a matter of time before the legitimacy of our participatory democratic settlement is seriously called into question. In these circumstances it's hard to believe that our present form of parliamentary democracy is sustainable.

In reaching our conclusions and recommendations I've been fortunate to have worked alongside a very talented group of journalists, communicators, politicians and academics, all of whom brought to the table an extraordinary degree of knowledge and commitment.

Our discussions were marked by a total absence of ideological baggage, and were motivated instead by a unanimous desire to place citizens, young and old, at the centre of the political food chain, rather than being left to pick up scraps at its fringes.

Earlier this year, during a debate in the House of Lords on the ability of Parliament to engage with the public, I made three points which seem worth repeating:

1. Parliament consistently fails to present itself as the sum of its parts. As a result, much of what is best gets submerged in broad-brush criticism of those areas in which it palpably fails to meet the expectations of the world outside.
2. Irrespective of the incremental improvements being made in almost all aspects of Parliament's work, the pace and, in some cases, the nature of change are failing to match that which is taking place in society at large. The result being that Parliament is not only failing to stay abreast of developments and opportunities but is, if anything, falling behind.
3. The level of informed, transparent and engaged democracy that any citizen of the 21st century has a right to expect is, of necessity, comparatively expensive. Cut-price democracy will never represent much of a bargain.

Unsurprisingly, almost all of our recommendations have budgetary implications but as we make clear in our Report, the costs involved, for example in creating an exemplary parliamentary website, must be regarded as an investment in modern democracy, not a charge against it.

We believe this new Parliament has the perfect opportunity to establish itself as being entirely capable of serving the interests of all the people of this country. Participation and an understanding of the process of government are a right, not a privilege. Here is a series of recommendations that, taken together, would have the effect of reconnecting Parliament with the people it exists to serve.

Lord Puttnam
Chair, Hansard Society Commission on the Communication of Parliamentary Democracy
6 May 2005

Executive Summary

A Voice for the People

A more effective Parliament would make a greater contribution than anything else to a renewal of British democracy. Parliament does not exist simply to provide Government with a majority and a mandate; it should also be a voice for the people – every day, not just once every four or five years.

But Parliament is simply not keeping pace with changes in society. So instead of the support and involvement of the public that Parliament requires, we see disengagement and cynicism, disappointing electoral turnout and low levels of satisfaction. Parliament is increasingly sidelined from the centre of British political life, with satire and neglect threatening to substitute for urgent or informed interest. If these trends continue the whole of our political and civic life will suffer.

The public have a right to expect a Parliament which communicates its work promptly, clearly and usefully, which reaches out to all citizens and which invites participation and interaction. Changes made by Parliament in recent years have not been far-reaching enough to meet its communication responsibilities in a rapidly-changing world. In the 21st century institutions that do not communicate fail. And in this Parliament is failing.

Failing the Public

Members of the public are increasingly turning to single issues rather than to parties and traditional political processes. Yet Parliament's communication is still predominantly organised around its own, often inward looking, procedures. In an environment in which people need to see how Parliament relates to the rest of our democracy and public debate, Parliament fails to link its work to other representative bodies and forums for discussing public issues. Where the public expect institutions to be responsive to their concerns, Parliament provides almost no opportunities for direct voter involvement, interaction or feedback. Where the public look for clear and readily accessible information, it remains unnecessarily difficult to find the information people need.

The Public Eye

Change should be driven by what citizens have a right to expect from their Parliament. Having listened to the public, parliamentarians, the media and interest groups during our inquiry, we have come to the following conclusions:

- The public have an absolute right to know what happens in Parliament, as well as a right to participate. The public should be able to understand proceedings, to contribute to inquiries and to access all forms of information about Parliament. This would entail a complete overhaul of Parliament's current communication structure

- Parliament should establish a Communications Service that brings together in a single department the various communication activities essential to a democratic institution. This department should develop a clear communication strategy founded on the widest consultation with the public and other interested bodies. The financial implications should not be seen as a cost, but as an investment in contemporary democracy

- The necessary overhaul of Parliament's communication structure will be incomplete without a change in the management of Parliament. Key steps are a House of Commons Commission made independent of the influence of the frontbenches; and the administration of the House of Commons by a Chief Executive, experienced in the management of complex organisations in the public realm

- Parliament should be accessible to the public – whether in London, in local regions, on television or via the internet. This means, for example, that unnecessary broadcasting restrictions should be removed; the website, which is confusing and poorly designed, should be radically improved; and visits to Parliament should offer significantly more than a heritage tour.

Parliament should be an accessible and readily understood institution, a Parliament that relates its work to the concerns of those in the outside world; and a media that works with Parliament to communicate effectively with the public. Parliament must be viewed through a far more engaged and informed public eye.

Our Recommendations

We urge all political parties to commit themselves to a renewal of British parliamentary life. The long-term gains for our democracy will be immense.

We believe a Parliament that involves and engages the public more effectively in its work, and where the public can exercise real influence, would respond to such increased attention with improved performance.

Parliament is currently failing in its democratic duty. Its organisation, procedures and general ethos are now seriously out of date. It has failed, in particular, to respond adequately to the opportunities provided by modern communications and in doing so has contributed to the growing alienation of the British public. Parliament may be serving its members more effectively, but there is yet to be a matching improvement in the service it provides to the public. Parliament needs to reassert itself, to reconnect with the public and become what it has always striven to be – the fountain of our democratic freedoms.

In order to achieve this, we make the following recommendations:

The Essentials of Modern Communications

R1   A Communications Service should be established for Parliament, bringing together within its departmental remit the various communication activities essential to a contemporary democratic institution [3.8]

R2   A single Joint Committee of both Houses should be established, responsible for communication matters, though MPs or Peers should be able to consider separately matters solely relevant to their respective Houses [3.14]

R3   A communication strategy for Parliament should be adopted, having been arrived at through a wide-reaching and open process of consultation with parliamentarians, the media, the public and other interested bodies [3.28]

R4   The communication strategy should take Parliament at least to 2010 with provision for a mid-term review, and it should be based on the optimum principles of accessibility and transparency; participation and responsiveness; accountability; inclusiveness; and best practice in management and communication [3.29]

R5   The communication strategy should be tabled for agreement by both Houses [3.30]

R6   The communication strategy will require regular reporting back to MPs and Peers, annual evaluation against targets, and provision for the public to participate in the evaluation process [3.31]

R7   The communication strategy must be accompanied by the necessary and long-term budgetary commitment from the parliamentary authorities. [3.37]

Elements of a Communication Strategy

R8　A new Communications Department should set up an advisory group of media representatives [4.6]

R9　Parliamentary officials should do much more to draw the media's attention explicitly to matters of public interest [4.12]

R10 The rules of television coverage in the chambers should be relaxed to allow, for example, appropriate reaction shots, the relevant use of close-ups, more panning shots of the backbenches and a greater range of coverage during divisions. It should be an explicit objective of parliamentary coverage to not just inform but to interest and engage the viewer [4.20]

R11 There should be a relaxation of the rules for filming in the precincts of Parliament, permission for walking shots, interviews with relevant persons other than MPs, and a wider interpretation of parliamentary subject-matter which genuinely reflects the richness of political activity taking place at any one time within Parliament [4.23]

R12 The ban on still photographs should be reconsidered in light of the communication principles set out above [4.24]

R13 The current restrictions on the number of passes available for media outlets should be reconsidered [4.26]

R14 The parliamentary authorities should provide regular, formal induction for journalists [4.27]

R15 A new Communications Department should establish effective processes to manage, edit, develop and continually update the parliamentary website [4.30]

R16 The parliamentary website should be radically improved. At a minimum, it should be consultative, interactive and easily navigable [4.43]

R17 An improved website should engage the widest range of citizens, using well-designed publicity and targeted advertising to help people understand that there is a virtual route through which they have easy access to their Parliament [4.44]

R18 Parliament should consider its role in consistently developing citizenship education resources and the different curriculum approaches across the UK. It should work closely with other organisations to support more training for teachers, and more and better materials for young people [4.50]

R19 Parliament's facilities, including the chambers, should be made available during recess for groups of young people [4.53]

R20 Parliament should take young people, including pre-voting citizens, far more seriously by involving them in its processes and decision-making [4.54]

R21 In line with recent joint recommendations from the Accommodation and Works Committee and Administration Committee, the Parliamentary Education Unit should have a well resourced and dedicated teaching space with multi-media facilities [4.61]

R22 Parliament should employ more full-time and contracted staff who are fully trained and experienced in working with young people in a range of different settings [4.62]

R23 A young persons' consultative group should be established with the right to attend and advise at key administrative meetings of both Houses [4.62]

R24 More should be done to enhance the effectiveness of parliamentary outreach work [4.63]

R25 There should be a thorough review of the language and terminology Parliament uses in accordance with our communication principles [4.69]

R26 Parliament should hold more meetings outside London. Select committees, for example, should hold more formal proceedings and public events beyond Westminster [4.73–4.74]

R27 All parliamentary procedures should be comprehensively reassessed from the perspective of the communication principles we have advocated [4.75]

R28 Parliament should revisit and implement the recommendations on topical debates put forward both by the Hansard Society Commission on Parliamentary Scrutiny (the 'Newton Commission') and by the Liaison Committee [4.78]

R29 The authorities in Parliament as they appoint staff, and the political parties as they select candidates, should recognise the need for greater diversity if Parliament is to function well. [4.79]

Media Coverage of Parliament

R30 A radical reform of parliamentary communication and presentation should provide an opportunity for the media to enhance their coverage of parliamentary business [5.12]

R31 There should be a renewed commitment by the commercial public service broadcasters to provide national and regional news and current affairs [5.16]

R32 We encourage all public service broadcasters to increase the quality and amount of political programming, particularly that designed to meet the needs of young people [5.20]

R33 The BBC must be required by the Department for Culture, Media and Sport and by Parliament to be explicit as to how it plans to report Parliament in an engaging, innovative and accessible way as part of its contribution to 'democratic value' [5.25]

R34 There should be greater integration between BBC Parliament and the broader spectrum BBC programming to improve cross trailing [5.27]

R35 Given the availability of webcasting of all parliamentary proceedings, the remit of BBC Parliament should be broadened to permit the live coverage of other noteworthy parliamentary hearings or debates [5.30]

R36 The 'democratic value' principles contained in the BBC's own Charter Renewal document imply the need for a significant increase in resources to BBC Parliament. BBC Parliament remains a seriously undervalued democratic and broadcasting resource, with immense potential to provide innovative parliamentary programming. The BBC should, in the coming months, provide a clear and substantial action plan for its development, and for a targeted and ambitious increase in its impact [5.31]

R37 Resources for BBC Parliament should not be at the expense of effective funding for high quality public service broadcasting on the main BBC channels. The BBC should continue to provide parliamentary coverage across the full range of its output, where it has the power to reach mass audiences. [5.32]

How Parliament Runs Itself

R38 We believe Parliament will communicate its own messages confidently and effectively only when it is administered independently of frontbench influence. We therefore propose that legislation be enacted to provide for the House of Commons Commission to be elected by secret ballot, with members of each party voting for a proportionate number of Commission members from among their number [6.6]

R39 We recommend that the administration of the House of Commons be headed by a Chief Executive, experienced in the management of complex organisations in the public realm, reporting directly to the House of Commons Commission. [6.11]

CHAPTER 1

INTRODUCTION: AN OVERVIEW

CHAPTER ONE
Introduction: an overview

A more effective Parliament would make a greater contribution than anything else to a renewal of British democracy. Parliament does not exist simply to provide Government with a majority and a mandate; it should also be a voice for the people – every day, not just once every four or five years.

Parliament is essential to the health of our democracy. To function effectively, Parliament requires the support and engagement of the public. But we see instead public disengagement and cynicism, with declining electoral turnout, low knowledge of, and satisfaction with, Parliament, and little information on Parliament available in the mainstream media. If this trend continues, the whole of our political and civic life will suffer.

The public have a right to expect a Parliament which communicates its work promptly, clearly and usefully, which reaches out to all citizens and invites participation and interaction. There is nothing utopian about these recommendations and while there has been some progress, Parliament still falls seriously short of achieving these ambitions.

Effective communication from Parliament can only increase understanding and appreciation of its work. Greater transparency will also be an incentive to improve performance in those areas where Parliament is currently failing. For all this to happen, however, Parliament must re-establish its own institutional identity, distinct from Government and the individual MPs and Peers who are its members.

1.1 Parliament faces a crisis of confidence, power and respect. It is taken less seriously than ever before by the media and the public. The Commons is losing influence in the country. Satire and neglect threaten to substitute for urgent or informed interest.

1.2 Our Commission on 'Parliament in the Public Eye' was set up by the Hansard Society to examine the communication of parliamentary democracy – how Parliament presents itself, and is presented by others, to the public.

1.3 Parliament is first and foremost a representative body and without clear communication there can be no adequate representation. This Report examines what 21st century communication looks like, what the public want and expect from those who claim to serve them, how Parliament is failing to relate to, let alone connect with, today's nation, and how it might start the process of reconnection.

1.4 Why does this matter? Because if people cannot understand what Parliament does, or why it does it, if people find its culture and language alienating, if voters cannot easily present their views and questions and believe they can make a difference, and if there is no continuing 'conversation' between Parliament and people, then Parliament cannot fulfil its purpose effectively.

1.5 We present this Report because we believe that without an effective Parliament our democracy is bound to fail. Government and media are not enough for a healthy modern society. Indeed, without Parliament, both the legitimacy of Government and the freedoms of the press are unlikely to stand.

1.6 The media are vital to the health of civic and political life. No other institution probes, reports and questions as effectively or reaches so many people; but the media are not, and do not claim to be, representative. That is Parliament's unique constitutional role at the heart of national politics.

1.7 Furthermore, a more effective Parliament improves the performance of Government. Vigorous and plural debate, and the testing and questioning of policy, not only improve the way in which ministers do their jobs but help to achieve public acceptance of governmental power.

1.8 Parliament is ideally placed to help resolve many of today's complaints and criticisms. It has the potential to offer plurality and diversity of viewpoint, a speedy response to emerging issues, a fast-moving policy debate taking place between equals, responsiveness to individual opinions, and authoritative decisions. Parliament has an essential role in ensuring a mature and balanced political discourse, reducing the danger of extreme and distorted solutions. No other body can offer this range of functions. Yet we are in danger of letting this essential democratic institution decline in public perception. Every other constitutional issue pales into insignificance beside this.

Parliament – in search of an identity?

1.9 To investigate how Parliament communicates is to come up immediately against a fundamental problem. What, or whom, do we mean by Parliament? There are, for a start, two autonomous chambers with distinct powers, administered separately. We can identify constitutional functions which they share and certain other functions they have agreed to exercise jointly. But to what extent, for the purposes of communication, are they a single Parliament as opposed to two Houses with differing approaches and aims in communication?

1.10 We examine in this Report the communication of both Houses of Parliament, and consider the extent to which it is desirable and feasible to achieve a single communication structure and strategy for Parliament encompassing both Houses. But we concentrate most of our attention on the House of Commons as the elected and representative chamber.

1.11 Not only should we ask whether Parliament is one or two institutions. Focusing on the House of Commons, we immediately come across three inter-related political realities – the Commons as 646 individuals, the Commons as a collection of political parties, and the Commons as a single political body voted in by the electorate to perform certain *parliamentary* functions. An MP from the Government party might one moment be in a select committee, exercising the parliamentary function of scrutinising the Executive, only to be interrupted by the division bell calling him or her to pass through the voting lobby as directed by the Government Whip, then ending the day dealing with the urgent casework of individual constituents.

1.12 It is vitally important to appreciate these three inter-related political realities of parliamentary life. First, there are the *646 individual MPs*, each of whom has his or her own political career. MPs have differing views as to the main purpose of being in Parliament (such as scrutinising the Executive, enacting or opposing a manifesto, representing constituents), and also their own views of communication. Voters continue to respect their local MPs and much of the effective communication of what Parliament does, especially at the local level and in the local media, is currently through the constituency Member. To over-emphasise Parliament as a single institution is to ignore the fact that MPs individually enjoy a high degree of independence in their communications with the public and are significantly more liked, trusted, and respected than Government, Parliament, political parties, and politicians in general.

1.13 A second identity available to MPs is that of their *party affiliation* and their relationship, be it of support or opposition, to the Government of the day. With no separation of powers, coverage and communication in Parliament can often simply mean communication by the Government and opposition parties (a cabinet minister making a statement in the chamber, for example).

1.14 Both of these identities – the individual constituency MP and the party politician – provide important opportunities for Parliament to communicate to the public. Websites, press articles, interviews in local media and blogs by local MPs, questions tabled or debates initiated by the parties to highlight their political positions: these all are fruitful and effective ways in which parliamentary work and its importance can be communicated. We are extremely supportive of such activity and encourage both local MPs and the political parties to use their communications and media access to convey the value of Parliament's work. But we cannot lose sight of the political realities facing individual MPs and political parties, and the fact that these operate on a different canvas from simply Parliament itself. Nor do they always operate in the best interests of Parliament.

1.15 In this Report we are mainly concerned with the third aspect: *Parliament as a political institution* in its own right, with its own particular functions and contribution to democratic life. These functions include:
   • the scrutiny of Government policies and actions
   • representing and communicating the views and interests of citizens
   • debating, approving or rejecting, and amending as appropriate, proposed legislation.

1.16 These distinct parliamentary functions must all be communicated if we are to secure greater public trust and involvement in our established democratic processes. But the evidence suggests that Parliament's constitutional role is not generally understood. To the public, Parliament is a location, a Palace, the theatre for ministerial and prime ministerial statements, the boxing ring for fights between Government and the Opposition. Parliament sums up and symbolises the whole concept of 'Westminster politics'. The distinction between Parliament and Government is not one that many outside Westminster understand and appreciate.

1.17 Remarkably, it was only in 1978 that the House of Commons (Administration) Act established some sort of corporate and legal identity for the elected chamber. But parliamentary candidates still stand on a manifesto which states only what their parties would hope to do in Government, not what they will do in Parliament. Parliament does not have an effective corporate identity – it is not even the sum of its parts.

1.18 The main responsibility to communicate Parliament's work must rest with Parliament itself. But Parliament will never communicate its work convincingly, never command the necessary resources nor develop the necessary strategy, if it lacks a distinct and confident institutional identity. This brings us to fundamental questions central to, but much wider than, our remit. In this Report we make radical recommendations on Parliament's administration, resourcing, communication strategy and on how Parliament engages with and involves the public. But we know that such changes will happen only if Government and the political parties – above all MPs and Peers themselves – make them happen.

1.19 **If our democracy is not to wither further, there has to be a rethinking of the place of Parliament in our political life. The newly elected Parliament provides a huge opportunity for all Members to take charge of change and re-establish the rights of Parliament.**

1.20 The development of a stronger and distinct parliamentary identity is in the interests of democracy as a whole. Government and political parties will also benefit. Certainly, as Parliament has become increasingly remote from the political and social expectations of the public over the last 25 years, so the wider reputation of politics over that same period has also suffered. **We urge all political parties to commit themselves to a renewal of British parliamentary life. The long-term gains for our democracy will be immense.**

The Powers and Independence of Parliament

1.21 Some of the submissions we received stated that Parliament could not hope to receive greater attention without having greater power in relation to the Executive. One form of such increased power occurs when the Government has a small majority or no majority at all. But there are also demands that the constitutional relationship between Government and Parliament be altered in such matters as the use of the Royal Prerogative, for example, when British troops are ordered into military action without the need for Parliament's consent.

1.22 Such consideration of the respective powers of Parliament and Government takes us beyond our brief. Of course, if Parliament gained in day-to-day power whether through reduced Government majorities, or by increased constitutional rights, there would be a corresponding increase in media and public attention. But our concern in this Report is to consider how – regardless of these issues – the public might be more involved and interested in the *parliamentary* activities carried out on their behalf: of scrutiny and debate, questioning and accountability. If the public lose interest in these democratic processes we believe the health of democracy inevitably suffers.

1.23 Other submissions called for Parliament to act more independently of Government and the political parties. This is less a question of granting new powers to Parliament than MPs, both individually and collectively, exercising its current powers more independently of party constraints. It is surprising that MPs still allow the frontbenches and whips to control the process by which Parliament's internal affairs are managed and directed. We call in this Report for Parliament to take back control of its own affairs from the whips.

1.24 We also received recommendations to reduce the number of whipped votes, to remove whips completely, to end the practice of nomination by the whips to membership of select committees. There were recommendations to reduce significantly the size of the payroll vote.[1]

1.25 These questions must be discussed realistically. Political parties remain at the heart both of Parliament and of the British political system. Any blueprint for Parliament which aims effectively to wish them away is neither workable, nor even desirable. Moreover, Parliament is acting more independently today than it has in past decades – if one is to judge independence by the number of backbench rebellions. Despite popular thinking, backbenchers have been more likely to rebel nowadays than in the past. The experience of select committees has also provided many examples of cross-party consensus criticising government policies and actions.

1.26 There is little doubt that, if MPs acted even more independently of party lines and frontbench pressures, Parliament would attract greater media and public attention. We believe MPs must reconsider whether they have yet achieved the right balance between the sometimes competing claims of Parliament and of party on their loyalty. Despite the increase in independently minded behaviour, this is not reflected accurately in the perceptions of the public and media. A visit to most standing committees at work would still reveal the worst influences of the party system on the functions of Parliament.

1.27 **We believe that a Parliament which involved and engaged the public more effectively in its work would respond to such increased attention with improved performance.** Professor Colin Seymour-Ure told us that, 'News media report Parliament if Parliament matters.'[2] Scrutiny, questioning, debate – these all matter when done well. We need the virtuous circle to be established – greater public attention leading to improved performance leading to further public engagement.

---

[1] This was also a recommendation of the Hansard Society Commission on Parliamentary Scrutiny: Hansard Society Commission on Parliamentary Scrutiny, *The Challenge for Parliament: Making Government Accountable* (Vacher Dod Publishing; London 2001)
[2] Professor Colin Seymour-Ure in evidence to the Commission

Our Inquiry

1.28 The Commission was set up by the Hansard Society in January 2004 to examine the communication of parliamentary democracy. More specifically, it looked at the presentation of Parliament; the effect of Parliament's procedures on publicising its work; the role of the media in explaining Parliament; and the potential of new channels of engagement. The terms of reference for the Commission can be found in Appendix 2.

1.29 Lord Puttnam chaired the Commission and was supported by vice-chair Jackie Ashley. Commissioners were drawn from the fields of media, politics and academia. The Commission benefited enormously from the wealth of knowledge and experience that each member brought to its deliberations. A list of members of the Commission and biographical information can be found in Appendix 1.

1.30 The Commission issued a call for written evidence to a wide range of individuals and organisations. We subsequently received 70 high quality submissions from parliamentarians, media organisations, youth groups, public affairs organisations, interest groups, members of the public and others. A complete list of contributors can be found in Appendix 3. In addition to this, the Commission obtained a substantial insight into parliamentary communications through a series of meetings and seminars.

1.31 Between May 2004 and November 2004 the Commission held 10 round-table seminars. These closed events enabled a broad range of views to be heard and so shaped the direction of the Commission. They were supplemented by speakers at Commission meetings held during 2004, including Sir Robert Phillis, Peter Kellner and Sir Bernard Crick. Appendix 4 lists events held by the Commission and individuals we met with.

1.32 The Commission organised a series of activities to consult the public. In addition to written evidence received from members of the public, the Commission organised, with the help of the Hansard Society's e-democracy programme, an online forum to examine the issues under consideration. This took the form of a 'Citizens' Panel' – as set out in Appendix 5. The 55 members of the 'Citizens' Panel' responded to a series of questions over a four-week period (October–November 2004). Their discussion and deliberation enabled the Commission to have sustained input from a public panel and to test its emerging recommendations. The Commission also held an event in Parliament in February 2005 for members of the public and other interested parties.

1.33 The Commission wanted continuous participation from young people and so a group was set up by the Carnegie Young People Initiative to follow the work of the Commission over its lifetime. Our inquiry greatly benefited from the insight, experience and contribution made by the Young People's Working Group. It was comprised of four people between the ages of 17 and 25. Members of the Group participated in a range of events, including an event specifically for young people; reviewed evidence received by the Commission; commented on our work, and drew up recommendations. More information can be found in Appendix 6.

Structure of the Report

1.34 In this Report we turn next to the widespread evidence of political disengagement, together with cultural, social and political trends and changes, which have left Parliament floundering in their wake. The Report then sets out the need for a Communications Department, a communication strategy and dedicated budget.

1.35 We go on to describe in more detail how Parliament currently organises its communication and how this communication might be improved. We look at how the public come across Parliament in the media, on the internet, in schools and the community and in visits to both Houses. We consider the implications for Parliament's proceedings of a commitment to far more effective engagement with the public.

1.36 The Report then discusses how media reporting of Parliament might be improved and the continuing obligations on public service broadcasters to inform and engage the public in Parliament's work.

1.37 An inescapable conclusion of our inquiry has been that Parliament's poor performance in its communications is part of its broader weakness as an organisation. We therefore end with a wider examination of how Parliament conducts its affairs and runs its own administration. We recommend a reform of the House of Commons Commission and the appointment of a Chief Executive for the House of Commons. These reforms will provide the independent political support and managerial expertise needed to support a modern Parliament in a fast-changing world.

CHAPTER 2

FAILING THE PUBLIC?

CHAPTER TWO
Failing the public?

There is widespread evidence of public disengagement from Parliament, in particular among young people, black and minority ethnic groups and other disadvantaged social groups. Such evidence includes low electoral turnout, poor levels of knowledge and trust, and media coverage which provides insufficient information on Parliament's work.

Parliament suffers from the wider detachment from 'traditional' politics but some of this disengagement is also a response to how Parliament currently presents itself to the public. Society has changed massively in recent years and the pace of change is set to accelerate, but Parliament is simply not keeping up.

Members of the public are increasingly turning to single issues rather than to parties and traditional political processes. But Parliament's communication is still organised around its own, often inward-looking, procedures. Where people need to see how Parliament relates to the rest of our democracy and public debate, Parliament fails to link its work to other representative bodies and forums for discussing public issues. Where the public expect institutions to be responsive to their concerns, Parliament provides almost no opportunities for direct voter involvement, interaction or feedback. Where the public look for clear and readily accessible information, it too often remains unnecessarily difficult to find the information people need.

2.1 The current relationship between Parliament and the public is essentially dysfunctional. Each side knows that somewhere along the line they have stopped communicating. A new relationship must be established in which people feel they are genuinely involved in the parliamentary process, that the debate is *their* debate. Democratic processes and institutions claim to act, and to draw their legitimacy, from citizens. Much of the evidence we received suggests that any sense of such commitment and engagement is declining, with possibly serious consequences for the longer-term health of the United Kingdom's political culture.

2.2 There is no simple measure of disengagement from political institutions. Rather, there are a range of indicators: levels of participation and action in the political process; levels of knowledge and interest; and levels of satisfaction and perceived efficacy. These factors were highlighted in recent Audits of Political Engagement by The Electoral Commission and the Hansard Society.[3] We believe they provide a comprehensive framework from which to assess attitudes towards Parliament.

Levels of participation

2.3 Electoral turnout is cited as one of the clearest indicators of disengagement from Parliament. Turnout in 2001 was just 59.7 per cent compared with 71.5 per cent in 1997. Turnout, of course, can go up as well as down and it can be hard to disaggregate short-term and long-term factors. But in the recent 2005 election, turnout remained at a consistently low level of 61 per cent. This average masks the particularly low turnout in a number of constituencies. The downward trend has been a feature of all parliamentary democracies in developed countries in recent years. Refusing or not bothering to vote may be as much a statement about the parties and Government, and a sign of a broader political detachment, as a view specifically of Parliament. But whatever the combination of causes, the fact of low electoral participation affects the status and health of Parliament. How far does electoral turnout have to drop before the legitimacy of the system is questioned? Even if legitimacy is not yet lost, at some point does Parliament lose the right to claim that it is in the House of Commons that the 'national conversation' takes place?

2.4 Election statistics show a recent, but serious, drop in participation among specific sections of society. For example, younger adults are not getting into the habit of voting as they grow older. Peter Kellner, Chair of YouGov, told us in June 2004 of a creeping and more firmly entrenched disengagement moving up the generations.

2.5 It should not be assumed that those who vote are fully or adequately engaged with our democratic processes. Recent polling by MORI finds that older generations have a more entrenched belief in the duty of voting and a more ingrained habit of turning out to the polls at a general election.[4] Duty and habit, while valuable qualities, do not, however, equate to hearts-and-minds participation. Such people are just as likely to be disappointed with the way Parliament is working as those who stay at home. This is the danger of relying solely on electoral turnout to judge detachment. Increased turnout does not necessarily equate to improved engagement.

---

[3] The Electoral Commission and the Hansard Society, *An Audit of Political Engagement* (The Electoral Commission and the Hansard Society; London 2004); and The Electoral Commission and the Hansard Society, *An Audit of Political Engagement 2*, (The Electoral Commission and the Hansard Society; London 2005)
[4] MORI in evidence to the Commission

2.6   Participation in politics cannot then solely be measured by levels of turnout in elections. Modern societies have a wide range of political activity beyond voting. Direct political activities include signing a petition, taking part in a demonstration, responding to a consultation or presenting views to an MP. Other activities, such as boycotting products, are a demonstration of political, social and ethical concerns and a willingness to act on them. These various activities are on the increase.

2.7   Many of these political activities relate directly to Parliament and are often intended to prompt a parliamentary response. The Electoral Commission and the Hansard Society's most recent Audit of Engagement found that one adult in six is a 'political activist' – defined as having done at least three from a list of eight political activities in the last two or three years.[5] Parliament should do more to engage with such alternative and wider political activity. While there is continuing evidence of disengagement from traditional and established politics, it appears that people have far from lost interest in the world around them and issues of importance.

Poor knowledge of Parliament

> *'Most of the population simply do not have a clue about how Parliament works or what our MPs do.'*[6]

2.8   It is impossible to value and engage with Parliament properly if you have little knowledge of its purpose, and surveys suggest considerable ignorance of how Parliament works. Indeed, recent focus groups conducted for the Hansard Society found that very few participants were able to discuss with any level of confidence how Parliament works or what is done there. One person commented, 'Nobody knows about Parliament except the people in Parliament.'[7] This is worrying given that levels of knowledge affect not only participation, but also attitudes towards an institution. The more people know – or think they know – about an organisation or an individual, the more favourable they tend to be towards it.[8]

2.9   The view that 'all politicians are the same' is a common belief that deters citizens from voting.[9] Some arrive at this conclusion from a politically informed standpoint. However, research has found that many believe this simply because they do not have sufficient information to distinguish

[5] The Electoral Commission and the Hansard Society, *An Audit of Political Engagement 2* (2005)
[6] Comment from member of the Commission's Citizens' Panel
[7] MORI, *Enhancing Engagement – Parliament and the Public: Research Study conducted for the Hansard Society* (MORI; London 2004)
[8] The Electoral Commission and the Hansard Society, *An Audit of Political Engagement* (2004)
[9] Milner, H., 'The Voters' Paradox: bringing back the knowledge dimension' (PSA Conference Paper; 2002)

between candidates or parties. Worryingly, it seems that this second group is on the rise and that this relates, in turn, to lower levels of turnout and to higher levels of disengagement from Parliament.

2.10 This mirrors evidence received by the Commission. Members of our Citizens' Panel, particularly younger participants, cited poor understanding as the reason behind their disengagement from Parliament: 'People feel alienated from politics simply because they do not understand it! I have peers who are undergraduates in top universities and in their early 20s yet who are completely ignorant about the workings of Parliament. Yet it is not through disinterest on their behalf but the lack of education that has led to this apathy. Through education comes understanding and people are far more likely to engage in politics and participate if they understand it.'[10]

2.11 The Daycare Trust found through consultations with disadvantaged parents across the country that there was a complete disengagement from political processes due to a lack of knowledge and confidence in participants' ability to make a difference.[11] MORI focus groups support this finding, with lack of knowledge of day-to-day activities in Parliament the most cited barrier to engagement. MORI found that few participants could discuss with any level of confidence how Parliament works or what goes on there.[12]

2.12 MORI polling has also charted how people perceive their knowledge of politics and Parliament.[13] In 2003 only 33 per cent said they knew 'a great deal' or 'a fair amount' about the way the Westminster Parliament works, with 67 per cent saying they knew 'a little/hardly anything' or 'had never heard of it/didn't know'. This is the lowest percentage claiming significant knowledge of Parliament since the question was first asked in 1991.

2.13 It is interesting to compare this percentage, relating to the Westminster Parliament, with the percentage of those claiming they know a great deal or fair amount about 'politics' – 42 per cent – and about the role of MPs – 45 per cent. It appears that people think themselves particularly ignorant of how Parliament works, even when compared with politics generally, or the work of individual MPs. Furthermore, since 1991 there has been a gradual upward trend in people's perceived knowledge of the European Union and local councils, in marked contrast with the decline recorded for the Westminster Parliament.

[10] Comment from member of the Commission's Citizens' Panel
[11] The Daycare Trust in evidence to the Commission
[12] MORI, Enhancing Engagement (2004)
[13] MORI in evidence to the Commission

2.14 MORI has been measuring how interested people say they are in politics for over 30 years, and has found the level remarkably stable.[14] For most of this period, around three in five people say they are at least fairly interested in politics, but this has dropped to half in MORI's latest research. Interest in local issues, national issues and international issues are all higher than in politics. Twice as many people are very interested in national issues than in politics and even more are very interested in local issues. Consequently, it is not that people are disengaged from the issues that surround them, but that they are failing to associate these concerns with the term 'politics' and with the work of the Westminster Parliament: 'There are people in our society who believe politics in no way affects their lives.'[15]

Low satisfaction with Parliament

2.15 The Audits of Political Engagement also assessed people's satisfaction with the political system and its institutions. Thirty-six per cent of respondents were satisfied with Parliament's performance, 32 per cent were dissatisfied and another 32 per cent expressed no opinion.[16] These averages mask a significant variation across social class and age, and a more modest variation between genders. 40 per cent of those aged over 55 were positive about Parliament, compared with only 28 per cent of 18 to 24 year olds, and there was a similar difference between middle- and working-class groups. The high proportion of respondents that expressed no opinion can be assumed to reflect the prevalence of low levels of understanding about Parliament.

2.16 Satisfaction is linked to trust. An overwhelming message from our evidence is a lack of trust in and identification with Parliament. One contributor to our Citizens' Panel concluded, 'The vast majority have no trust whatsoever in politicians.'[17] Distrust in the national Parliament has often been higher in the UK than for most of Europe. A 2004 poll of the 15 (at the time) Member States of the European Union [EU] found that 61 per cent of UK respondents said they did not trust their national Parliament, compared with an EU average of 54 per cent.[18] Gender and education were both factors in levels of trust, with 29 per cent of men tending to trust Parliament compared with 20 per cent of women; 21 per cent of those educated to age 15 or under tended to trust Parliament, compared with 42 per cent of those educated to 20 or beyond.

---

[14] MORI in evidence to the Commission
[15] Comment from member of the Commission's Citizens' Panel
[16] The Electoral Commission and the Hansard Society, *An Audit of Political Engagement* (2004)
[17] Comment from member of the Commission's Citizens' Panel
[18] European Opinion Research Group, *Standard Eurobarometer 61/Spring 2004: Public Opinion in the EU15*, (Directorate General Press & Communications; 2004)

On a more positive note, the most recent polling reports a drop in the proportion of the UK public who do not trust Parliament – down to 54 per cent.[19]

2.17 In contrast, most people do trust their local MP. Forty-one per cent said they were satisfied with their local MP in 2003, and this figure has remained almost constant since 1991 (43 per cent); while those saying they are dissatisfied has declined from 23 per cent in 1991, to 13 per cent in 2003.[20] Satisfaction seems to relate closely to whether people have had contact with their MP and whether they know their MP's name. While there are no differences in views between men and women or by social class for this indicator, ethnicity is a key factor: 42 per cent of white people are satisfied with their MP compared with 30 per cent among those from black and minority ethnic groups.[21] The relatively high satisfaction with individual MPs does not translate, however, into satisfaction with MPs generally.

People are more likely to be engaged if they think that 'getting involved works'

2.18 Over two-fifths of the public (41 per cent) disagree with the statement that, 'When people like me get involved in politics, they can change the way that the country is run', 36 per cent agree with it and one in five expresses no opinion either way.[22] Perceptions of the efficacy of participation have been found to be closely linked to other attitudinal measures, such as levels of interest in politics and perceived knowledge and opinions of how the system of Government works.

2.19 MORI found that a feeling of 'not being listened to' prevents the public from engaging with Parliament.[23] Thus, when people do feel informed about a political issue and want to make their views known, there is a general sense that it is a waste of time to do so. As one person commented, 'Individually, you've got no chance of changing anything.'[24]

Parliament's declining media profile

2.20 In a MORI survey 52 per cent of respondents considered the media to be one of the three institutions with the most impact on people's lives (compared with

---

[19] European Opinion Research Group, *Standard Eurobarometer 62/Autumn 2004: Public Opinion in the EU* (Directorate General Press & Communications; 2005)
[20] MORI in evidence to the Commission
[21] The Electoral Commission and Hansard Society, *An Audit of Political Engagement* (2004)
[22] Ibid.
[23] MORI, *Enhancing Engagement* (2004)
[24] Male, Stockport, younger in MORI, *Enhancing Engagement* (2004)

only 30 per cent for the Westminster Parliament).[25] While trust in the press is not that high, public service broadcasters continue to enjoy high levels of trust. In the recent survey of public attitudes towards conduct in public life, published by the Committee on Standards in Public Life, 82 per cent of respondents said that television news shapes their views, the most frequently cited influence by a wide margin.[26] The media remain a vital factor in informing and engaging people with Parliament's work.

2.21 It is clear that satisfaction with Parliament could be significantly increased by greater knowledge of its activity. But our evidence was of declining coverage in our national newspapers. Ralph Negrine writes of, 'the paucity of information about Parliament and its work which is currently available in the general news media'.[27]

2.22 Studies of the number of items in newspapers with a parliamentary connection reveal the impact of the demise of the 'parliamentary page' in broadsheet newspapers. Recent attempts by three papers to revive their parliamentary pages have not lasted long and there is little point in dreaming of their return. It would in any event be a mistake to think of such coverage as a 'golden age' of parliamentary reporting. While such reports may well have catered for a restricted group needing to know as soon as possible about key debates, they probably did little to inform the wider population about the work of Parliament: 'in reality the reports were exclusive, often unreadable and largely unread except by those who hoped to be quoted in them'.[28] In our age, when *Hansard* is available the next day on the web, the case for such reporting is all but dead.

2.23 Ralph Negrine makes the point that, 'In the newspapers of 1966, there were many small items of news – within the paper and on the parliamentary page – whose newsworthiness would, at least by today's standards, be dubious. In other words, we might also wish to question whether all the items that made up the totality of parliamentary and political coverage in the past were deserving of attention.'[29]

2.24 The decline in the amount of coverage in the press is related both to a change in the position of Parliament in British public life and different tests of newsworthiness in today's media. It must also be seen in the context of

[25] The Electoral Commission and the Hansard Society, *An Audit of Political Engagement* (2004)
[26] Committee on Standards in Public Life, *Survey of public attitudes towards conduct in public life*, (Committee on Standards in Public Life; London 2004)
[27] Dr Ralph Negrine in evidence to the Commission
[28] Alan Rusbridger, Editor of *The Guardian*, in evidence to the Commission
[29] Ralph Negrine in evidence to the Commission

a more general decrease in political coverage. There is less information about Parliament communicated to the public by the media, and that which does get through is strongly determined by an increasingly sensationalist news culture and does not remotely reflect the variety of parliamentary work. Even where Parliament continues to be reported on the public service broadcasting channels, there is evidence that television, like the press, concentrates on a few Government and frontbench MPs, with limited coverage of the political engagement of other backbenchers.[30]

Political and social trends

2.25 British society and politics have changed enormously in the past few decades and there is every reason to believe that most of these trends will continue. But Parliament has simply not kept up. If our representative body becomes an anachronism our democracy suffers. In this section we identify the main social and political trends which challenge the way in which Parliament currently operates.

People remain strongly engaged with political, social and ethical issues, but there has been a decline in identification with political parties.

2.26 Does the disengagement described in the introduction mean that the public have no interest in political life? Were that true, it would be hard to see how Parliament could begin to re-establish a relationship with the British people. But we were told repeatedly that people were turned off 'Westminster' politics and political institutions, but remained engaged with political and ethical issues. In the last two years Britain has seen some of the largest political demonstrations in its history, but these focused on particular issues (the countryside, war in Iraq) rather than a particular party.

2.27 As previously stated, The Electoral Commission and the Hansard Society Audits of Political Engagement found that, while there has been a decline in the proportion of people expressing an interest in politics, there remains a very real interest in political issues, and an aspiration to have a say in how the country is run.

2.28 The contrast between continuing engagement with issues but detachment from Westminster politics is illustrated by the fact that two in five of the public have donated money or paid a membership fee to a charity or campaigning organisation, while only one in 20 has paid to join a political

---

[30] Ibid

party or donated money to one (see Figure 1).[31] While party membership has declined dramatically from its peak in the 1950s (see Figure 2), membership of, for example, Greenpeace and Friends of the Earth has increased ten-fold since 1981.[32]

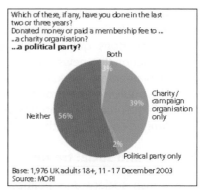

Which of these, if any, have you done in the last two or three years?
Donated money or paid a membership fee to ...
..a charity organisation?
...a political party?

Base: 1,976 UK adults 18+, 11 - 17 December 2003
Source: MORI

Figure 1: Political membership and giving

2.29 The kind of party politics we now see at Westminster is not considered either relevant or attractive by most of the public. MPs tend to be seen as engaged for much of the time in the small world where party point-scoring is the main activity. Hopefully, our Report provides a 'reality check'. This continuing interest in 'issues' is an important route through which Parliament can re-engage the public. The subject-based select committees are one means through which such

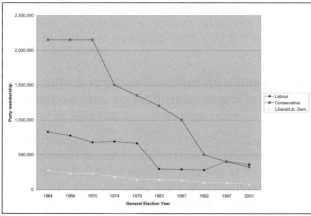

Figure 2: Party membership

issue-based politics might be developed. But at present, amazingly, it is not possible to search the parliamentary website by 'issues' (for example, to find out what has been happening around climate change), nor can one easily receive subject-specific information from Parliament.

2.30 For the most part, Parliament is seen by the public simply as a battle ground between the parties, each aiming to increase its seats at the next election. This is not a politics which attracts the interest or respect of a vast majority of the British people. As Robin Cook MP said, 'The tribal character of party

---

[31] The Electoral Commission and Hansard Society, *An Audit of Political Engagement* (2004). Figure 14: Political membership and giving.

[32] POWER Inquiry, *Commission Research Paper - The decline in political participation and involvement in Britain: an introduction*, (POWER; London, 2005)

politics may now be a trap for Parliament. The world outside Parliament has changed ... The challenge to the Commons is whether we can adjust to the less tribal society, which we are supposed to represent.'[33]

Parliament now has to 'compete' with a number of other political bodies and processes – such as the devolved assemblies, the EU institutions, the rise of judicial review and think-tanks – if it is to attract attention.

2.31 There has also been a fundamental change in the role of Parliament within our political life. Better communication and improved engagement will not restore Parliament to a monopoly position, which some nostalgically regret. Nor would we necessarily want that. If we believe in people relating effectively to those bodies which represent them, this must go beyond the Westminster Parliament to include local authorities, devolved and regional assemblies, and the European Parliament.

2.32 The Editor of *The Guardian*, Alan Rusbridger, made the point persuasively, 'The truth is that Parliament is often only a backdrop to a political game played elsewhere. In a world of devolution, judicial review, think-tanks, the European Union, rolling broadcast news and the *Today* programme, the House of Commons can struggle to get noticed. That is a reflection of reality. In news terms, *when* and *what* almost always outweighs *where*. A prime ministerial comment in the street or in a press conference often counts for as much as a prime ministerial comment in the chamber.'[34]

2.33 The Electoral Commission told us that, 'One particular challenge facing Parliament in communicating its work is that it is increasingly operating in a "crowded market". Someone in Scotland is now represented by 18 different elected representatives, rising to 19 in areas with community councils. Communicating the respective jurisdictions and performance of these institutions – and Parliament's role within the "mix" – represents a significant challenge.'[35]

2.34 Added to this is a Government which every day communicates directly to the media and public. The Government uses its immense resources to communicate and consult with citizens. Even Whitehall has opened up, though maybe not enough, to the media and public. Policy debates on almost every level are vigorously pursued by a host of think-tanks, NGOs and

---

[33] Rt Hon Robin Cook MP, Hansard Society Annual Lecture 2002
[34] Alan Rusbridger in evidence to the Commission
[35] The Electoral Commission in evidence to the Commission

voluntary organisations. The debate in the chamber is often just a repetition of arguments rehearsed extensively beforehand in conferences, seminars, media studios and public events.

2.35 Further, many of the key challenges facing us require global solutions. Whether it is climate change, HIV, conflict resolution, migration, terrorism – the international mobilisation of resources and political will required to address such issues dwarfs the powers of any national Parliament. Nevertheless, Parliament has a key role to play and should do more to convey the way in which its work can make a difference. But more often than not this role is one of lobbying, persuasion and co-operation, rather than the long-lost imperial model of a Parliament whose writ held sway around the world.

2.36 All these facts of political life cannot and should not be wished away. Many involve increased opportunities for political engagement and information. Parliament cannot look back wistfully to its former pre-eminence, but now has to go out and make its case for attention and involvement. It requires a clear and agreed sense of its true 'added value' to the political process.

2.37 Parliamentary communication should be planned as part of the broader political reality. There must, for example, be consideration of how Parliament's work can be communicated in a way which links up with the activity of both the Government and other democratic institutions. At present, the parliamentary website gives little sense of the activities and functions of other representative bodies, such as the Scottish Parliament, National Assembly for Wales, or local authorities.

Important changes have taken place within Parliament, with the most effective activity moving away from the chamber to the committee corridor, Portcullis House and the offices of individual MPs.

2.38 Even within Parliament itself, the focus and energy of political life has moved from the chamber to committees. Since the current system of select committees was established in 1979, their work has steadily increased in impact and reputation. Many of those we spoke to contrasted select committees and pre-legislative scrutiny committees with a chamber 'either rowdy or empty', and with standing committees, which are politically driven and whose purpose is the amendment of Bills, but which were generally seen as failing to deliver much in the way of effective scrutiny.

2.39 Just as the work of select committees has expanded and is receiving increasing publicity, there has been a similarly large increase in the postbag and workload of the individual MP. 'All-party groups' have also grown in number at Westminster and, while they vary in size and activity, the more lively exert real influence in their subject areas.

2.40 Not only must Parliament renegotiate its place in political life, but there also needs to be a recognition that the Commons chamber has, for the most part, ceased to be effective or central to scrutiny. Select committees, the representations of individual MPs and the work of all-party groups all continue to scrutinise, question and represent on behalf of voters. Far more could be done to communicate the range of parliamentary activity which continues to make a difference to people's lives.

2.41 The continuing emphasis of broadcasters on the chamber and most particularly on Prime Minister's Questions gives a greatly distorted image of Parliament. The aim of the Commons' authorities to increase coverage of select committees is welcome. To that should be added consideration of how to publicise the broad range of informal parliamentary activity.

The development of a rights-based political culture and a less deferential society.

2.42 There is a growing awareness of an individual's identity and rights as a citizen. This has partly been mirrored in policy and legislation. The Human Rights Act brought the provisions of the European Convention on Human Rights within the ambit of British law. Equality and anti-discrimination legislation has been developed and extended in a number of areas. Embryonic rights to information are found in the recently implemented Freedom of Information Act.

2.43 The right to know, the right to be heard, the right to be treated equally, the right to be served well by the political process, these are all demands to which a modern Parliament has to respond. A sample quotation, summarising opinions expressed during the BBC's research into public disillusion with politics, is typical of much we heard during our inquiry, 'Parliament lacks a contemporary personality. It's seen as boring, old fashioned and formal, dating from a deferential age when people would stop and listen to those "better and wiser". For younger groups, time-honoured procedures communicate not revered tradition, but a refusal to accept that times change. Furthermore, they no longer feel respect for Parliament but morally superior to those who seem to have forgotten that they are there to serve the people.'[36]

---

[36] BBC, *Beyond the Soundbite* (2002)

2.44 Much in that quotation might be unfair or excessive. But perceptions matter. Parliament is no longer taken on trust, no longer deferred to. It has continually to make its case and prove itself worthy of the citizen's consideration. Parliament has to present itself as an institution which can serve and further the individual's democratic rights. Parliament has to re-think itself as a service provider to citizens and identify what citizens can and should legitimately be demanding of it.

The rise of consumerism affects all aspects of life – the public have expectations of a customer-focused approach, of speed of delivery, of choice and of the ability to specify needs and complain when they are not met. The performance of individuals and institutions are assessed and evaluated against transparent standards.

2.45 The emphasis in a market-led economy on the consumer, and the changes in customer service introduced in recent years, have resul-ted in people being much clearer as to the kind of service they want as well as, conversely, what they are not prepared to accept.

Copyright Hansard Society

2.46 Consumers increasingly expect service at their own convenience, not at the convenience of the provider. We are increasingly critical of any situation in which we appear to be at the mercy of a monopoly supplier.

2.47 The BBC's research found that in a fast-moving world a vote every four years is perceived as a 'poor deal', even archaic, by today's consumer-savvy electorate.[37] People are increasingly using consumer values and ideas to evaluate their relationship with politics and politicians, for example, choice, service, accountability. Many people were clearly influenced in their view of politics by consumer culture. It is second nature to them that the customer is always right and the consumer is accustomed to expecting efficiency, quality, service and accountability from the 'brands' it trusts.

---

[37] Ibid.

2.48 Both the public and private sectors have also developed an emphasis on performance management, independent evaluation of success, accountability for poor performance and the need to deal effectively with complaints from clients/customers/citizens. This culture of accountability seems to have passed Parliament by. While there are annual reports from the House of Commons Commission on aspects of parliamentary administration, there is no corporate sense of what an effectively performing Parliament would look like.

2.49 Many of these disciplines, which other institutions and individuals are so familiar with, and which Parliament so often demands of others, are perfectly applicable to Parliament itself. However, Parliament often appears to have exempted itself from the expectations common elsewhere in our society.

Media culture is changing and is further influenced by the impact of new technologies.

2.50 Parliament has slipped many years behind current developments in digital information and communication. Indeed its recent history has always been of adapting to new technologies years, sometimes decades, after their introduction in the rest of society. Television is an obvious example. Colin Seymour-Ure pointed out to us that the cinema newsreel passed Parliament by completely.[38] Perhaps Parliament's political capital allowed it to do so in the past, but it can do so no longer.

2.51 New technologies have multiplied the diversity, flexibility, quantity and immediacy of communication. We have a more entertainment- and media-based culture, higher expectations about speed of decision-making, much greater access to information, and ever more participation and direct communication without the need for intermediaries. There are implications for the future of the media and of politics with the rise of peer-to-peer news reporting and self-initiated virtual communities engaging with particular issues or wider political campaigns.

2.52 But technology is only part of the story. People are no longer content to be observers of a debate and a process which claims to be taking place on their behalf. Political debate has been democratised and Parliament must acknowledge and catch-up with it.

---

[38] Professor Colin Seymour-Ure in evidence to the Commission

2.53 Declining participation in elections, and low knowledge of, and satisfaction with, Parliament are all linked to Parliament's increasing remoteness from the world in which most people are living. Ease of access, clarity, responsiveness and services aimed to meet specific requirements, these have become commonplace expectations. In failing to keep up with such trends in society, Parliament is short-changing the public it claims to serve. In the remainder of this Report we set out how such failings can be addressed.

CHAPTER 3

THE ESSENTIALS OF MODERN COMMUNICATIONS

CHAPTER THREE
The essentials of modern communications

Parliament has in the last few years made real and significant improvements to its communication with the public. But they have not been far-reaching enough to meet its communication responsibilities in a fast-changing world. Radical change is required, starting from first principles, as to what citizens have a right to expect from their Parliament.

To meet the rights of the public to accurate and comprehensive information, Parliament requires the same communications resource as that enjoyed by other significant public organisations. Instead of the current diffuse and complex distribution of responsibilities, there should be a single communications system, rooted in a department responsible for all aspects of external communication and with a dedicated budget. With these in place, a strategy can be developed which sets out a clear and comprehensive plan to re-engage the public with Parliament's work.

'The Commons Information Office is a useful, if little known, source of guidance but there is no obvious point of access for journalists and the wider public to discover what is happening at Westminster, what is about to happen and what might be of interest to them ... There is no Westminster counterweight to the government communications machine – which provides more than 50 press officers at some large domestic departments.'[39]

3.1 At present the main Commons departments are organised around officials whose posts were established centuries ago, such as the Clerk of the House or the Serjeant at Arms. To them have been added more recently some departments, such as Finance and Administration or Refreshment, more typical of a modern organisation. It would, however, be hard to find any other significant institution with a need to communicate with the outside world as one of its 'core tasks' which does not have a Communications Department.

3.2 There have been improvements to the organisation of parliamentary communication. Both Houses have begun to acknowledge that the communication of Parliament's work should be handled by professionals.

---

[39] *The Guardian* in evidence to the Commission

3. The essentials of modern communications

The first Director of Public Information for the House of Lords and a Communication Adviser for the House of Commons have both been important appointments (in 1996 and 2000 respectively). These developments have been welcomed. We also heard praise for the introduction of select committee media officers who seem to be increasingly effective. These appointments, however, cannot be said to constitute a 'Communications Department'.

3.3 The Modernisation Committee in its Report on *Connecting Parliament and the Public* called for 'the establishment of a central press office for the House of Commons, to take a more pro-active role in promoting the House and its work'.[40] The Committee cited the example of the National Assembly for Wales which has a Public Information and Education Service. As the example implies, what is needed is not just a press office, but a single Communications Department that has responsibility for all aspects of Parliament's communication. This would mean that the services currently delivered by, for example, the Commons Information Office, the Lords Information Office, the Parliamentary Education Unit, the Communications Adviser and media officers, the Central Tours Office, the Broadcasting Unit and Parliamentary Recording Unit, and those responsible for the website, are all provided from within a single department.

3.4 The Scottish Parliament has already consolidated its communication activity in exactly this way. The Modernisation Committee was told in evidence that, 'In 2003 the Scottish Parliament created an Access and Information Directorate, bringing together their "outward facing" offices together with information services. The new Directorate comprises the Parliament's Media Relations Office, Broadcasting, Security, Research and Information Services, Corporate Publications and Participation Services which covers Education and Outreach, participation events, public enquiry handling, and public information and visitor services. The creation of the Directorate reflects the Scottish Parliament's continuing commitment to live up to one of its key founding principles of openness, accessibility and participation.'[41]

3.5 With such a department many of the requirements for parliamentary communication would fall into place – a department clearly responsible for consultation on the drafting and implementation of a strategy; an adequate,

---

[40] House of Commons Select Committee on Modernisation of the House of Commons, *Connecting Parliament with the Public: First Report of Session 2003-04* (2004), HC 368
[41] Ibid.

transparent and accountable communication budget; a cadre of communication professionals working alongside procedural experts; an authoritative voice within Parliament's administration which can comment on the communication significance of all aspects of parliamentary activity; and an identifiable point of contact for media and the public. The current system fails to provide any of these essential elements.

3.6 At present the administration of parliamentary communication is extremely confusing, with the management of different aspects of communication dispersed across various separate departments. The Communications Adviser and media officers in the Commons come within the Office of the Clerk; the Parliamentary Education Unit and the Information Office are in the Commons Library; responsibility for the website remains diffuse and unclear; the Central Tours Office comes within the Department of the Serjeant at Arms, as does the Parliamentary Communications Directorate, whose only external communication responsibilities relate to the running of the parliamentary switchboard. All of these services also operate on behalf of the House of Lords, apart from the Information Offices, the Commons Communications Adviser and select committee media officers.

3.7 In an attempt to compensate for this diffuse structure an advisory body has been established, the Group on Information for the Public, or GIP, consisting of senior officials from all relevant Commons departments and also including the Director of Information from the House of Lords. GIP is charged by the Board of Management 'with developing policy and coordinating activities' in the areas of public understanding and access.

3.8 GIP meets about once a month. Its budget, held by the Office of the Clerk, for public information materials and customer research amounts to £55,000 a year. It does not have any executive powers nor the authority to identify and champion substantial reform. GIP has done important work in areas such as webcasting and visitor facilities, but much of its work appears to be reactive to external initiatives, be it House committees or bodies outside Parliament. While this is a useful role, it does not come close to meeting the proactive requirements of a Communications Department as outlined above. **We recommend that a Communications Service be established for Parliament, bringing together within its departmental remit the various communication activities essential to a contemporary democratic institution.**

3. The essentials of modern communications

3.9 In various areas the House of Lords already shares in communication arrangements administered by the House of Commons. We accept that there are some aspects of communication which are specific to each House and that may call for distinct units within a single department, for example, separate media officers to ensure that the Lords is not denied appropriate attention.

3.10 Joint working and shared resources are essential if Parliament, and parliamentary functions, are to be communicated effectively to the public. The perspective of the public, of the citizen, is the important one. This requires coordination and consistency in the manner in which the work of Parliament is communicated across both Houses.

Accountability to parliamentarians

3.11 There seems to be little understanding among parliamentarians of current communication structures. But without such political engagement and support, officials will, quite understandably, only ever propose minor and incremental change. The question of political accountability for Parliament's communication is a difficult one. Government communication can at root be reduced to the views and direction of a single person, the Prime Minister. The House of Commons has 646 Members, and there are about a further 700 in the Lords, all with their own perspective on how Parliament should function. It is vital that Parliament's communication is ultimately controlled by the Members themselves rather than being primarily the work of officials. A system is needed which can provide genuine consultation, information and accountability for parliamentarians while at the same time delivering efficient decision-making. Officials need knowledgeable and committed political support to implement real and meaningful change.

3.12 At the end of this Report we make some recommendations on the involvement of MPs in the general administration of the House of Commons. Involvement of parliamentarians in communication is at the moment principally achieved through the domestic select committees. There are a number of such committees which claim responsibility for various aspects of communication. In the Commons there is the Broadcasting Committee, the Information Committee, the Administration Committee, the Accommodation and Works Committee,[42] and now the Modernisation Committee; in the Lords there is the House Committee and the Information Committee.

[42] The Information Committee, Administration Committee, Accommodation and Works Committee and Catering Committee are collectively known as the Domestic Committees and governed by Standing Order No.140

Each was set up at a different stage of parliamentary development and reform. None has comprehensive responsibility for communication matters and there is overlap between their remits.

3.13 Visitor facilities, for example, have been reported on by the Lords' House Committee and by the Accommodation and Works and Administration Committees in the Commons. They were also discussed by the Modernisation Committee as part of a wider review of communication between Parliament and the public. The Broadcasting Committee is responsible, under powers delegated from the Speaker, for deciding on the rules of coverage in the Commons chamber, Westminster Hall and other public proceedings. It is the Administration Committee, however, which decides on other 'access points' for broadcasters in the precincts of the Palace and on the rules which should apply.

3.14 **We recommend that there be a single Joint Committee of both Houses responsible for communication matters, though MPs or Peers should be able to consider separately matters solely relevant to their respective Houses.** The Committee would advise the House of Commons Commission and the House Committee in the Lords on the work of the Communications Department, have delegated responsibility to determine rules for broadcasting and filming, undertake inquiries to gather views on best practice and how Parliament's performance might be improved and act as a channel of communication between the parliamentary authorities and MPs and Peers. It would also be a clear point of contact for members of the public who wished to raise communication concerns. Once the broad parameters have been agreed, the current role of the Finance and Services Committee to consider issues with budgetary implications could be maintained.

3.15 We set out in the diagrams below an attempt to capture the current arrangements for external communications, along with our proposed reformed system.

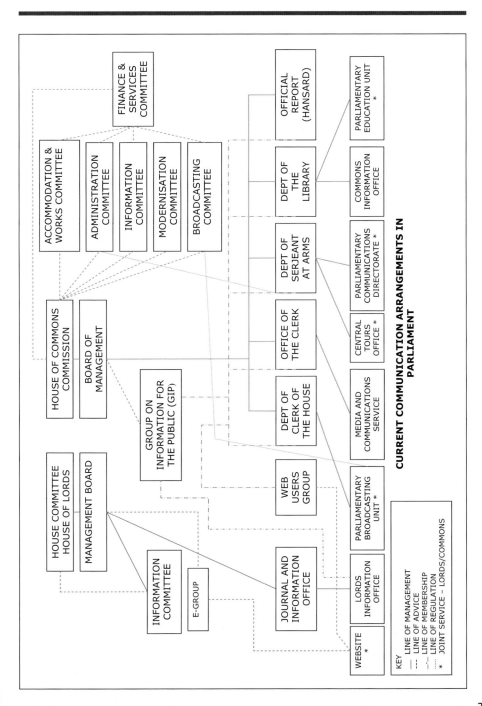

CURRENT COMMUNICATION ARRANGEMENTS IN PARLIAMENT

KEY
— LINE OF MANAGEMENT
-- LINE OF ADVICE
-·- LINE OF MEMBERSHIP
···· LINE OF REGULATION
* JOINT SERVICE – LORDS/COMMONS

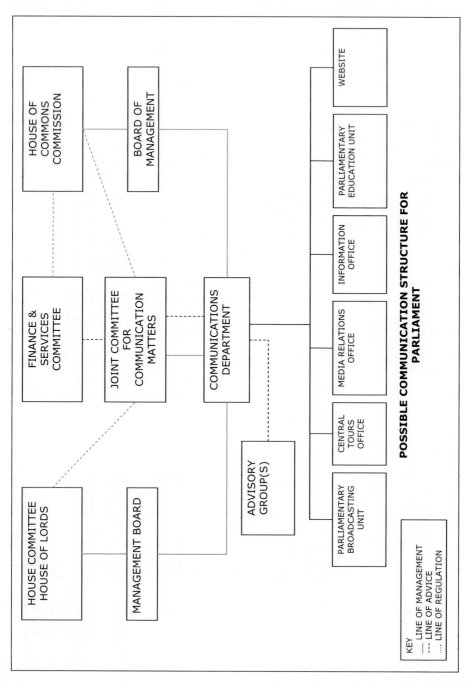

POSSIBLE COMMUNICATION STRUCTURE FOR PARLIAMENT

HOUSE OF COMMONS COMMISSION

BOARD OF MANAGEMENT

FINANCE & SERVICES COMMITTEE

JOINT COMMITTEE FOR COMMUNICATION MATTERS

COMMUNICATIONS DEPARTMENT

HOUSE COMMITTEE HOUSE OF LORDS

MANAGEMENT BOARD

ADVISORY GROUP(S)

WEBSITE

PARLIAMENTARY EDUCATION UNIT

INFORMATION OFFICE

MEDIA RELATIONS OFFICE

CENTRAL TOURS OFFICE

PARLIAMENTARY BROADCASTING UNIT

KEY
— LINE OF MANAGEMENT
--- LINE OF ADVICE
.... LINE OF REGULATION

3. The essentials of modern communications

A Communication Strategy

3.16 A number of principles should drive all of Parliament's communication with the public, namely:

i Accessibility and Transparency
Accessibility requires Parliament to maximise the ability of the public to attend or observe its proceedings, and obtain information. Transparency requires Parliament to ensure that its purpose, proceedings and means of engagement are made clear to all.

ii Participation and Responsiveness
Participation requires Parliament to provide, throughout its work, opportunities and encouragement for the public to engage with its proceedings so as to express their views, ask questions, respond to proposals and suggest initiatives. Responsiveness requires Parliament not only to listen but also to respond, and to initiate and engage in constructive discussion with the public.

iii Accountability to the public
Accountability requires Parliament to ensure that its performance is consulted upon, planned, explained and evaluated on a continuing basis.

iv Inclusiveness
Inclusiveness requires Parliament to ensure in all its proceedings and communication that the diversity of the British public – for example, in age, ethnicity, location, knowledge, gender, sexuality, and disability – is addressed and reflected.

v A model of good practice in management and communication
To be a model of good practice requires Parliament to apply best practice, creativity and initiative in management, communication and engagement, continually learning from as wide a range of sources as possible.

3.17 Hansard Society Scotland pointed to the principles adopted by the Scottish Parliament – sharing the power; accountability; access and participation; equal opportunities – as important in defining the new approach of that assembly.[43] When we visited the Scottish Parliament, we were told by a number of people, and could see ourselves, that these principles had a real impact on the life and decision-making of the Parliament. All four principles have an effect at every level on communication and participation, from the reception visitors receive when they enter the campus, to new procedures, such as that for Public Petitions, which provide genuine opportunities for engagement.

---

[43] Hansard Society Scotland in evidence to the Commission

3.18 The third principle, 'access and participation', is of particular relevance: 'The Scottish Parliament should be accessible, open, responsive and [should] develop procedures which make possible a participative approach to the development, consideration and scrutiny of policy and legislation.'[44] This principle has ensured that the relationship with the public is not just an 'add-on' but integral to all the Scottish Parliament's work.

3.19 The Commons Information Select Committee drafted a set of principles for the use of information and communications technology (ICT) in their report *Digital Technology: Working for Parliament and the Public*.[45] As well as assisting Members in carrying out their work in the Commons, the Committee sought to enable the public to engage more fully with the work of the House. In doing so, the Committee recognised the importance of a communication strategy that: maximises the accessibility and transparency of Parliament; enhances the professionalism of Members and staff in all aspects of parliamentary life; uses ICT to increase public participation in the work of the Commons; recognises the value of openness and uses ICT to enable public access to proceedings and papers; and develops and shares good practice. The House of Commons Commission agreed that the Committee's five principles should be taken into account in its strategic plan.

3.20 The recommendations of the Commons Information Committee are an important first step. However, they neither aim nor claim to be a comprehensive set of principles to govern Parliament's communication with the public, such as those which we have set out above.

3.21 The submission from the House of Lords' Director of Public Information states that the Lords has an 'aim' to 'improve and increase public understanding and knowledge of the role and work of the House'.[46] The House of Commons Commission adopted an outline strategic plan in October 2001 which defined four core tasks for the House service, one of which is 'providing information and access for the public'.[47]

3.22 This core task has been translated into a development objective for 2001-2006, 'to improve public understanding and knowledge of the work of the House and to increase its accessibility, subject to the requirements of security'.

---

[44] Ibid.
[45] House of Commons Information Committee, *Digital Technology: Working for Parliament and the Public. First Report of Session 2001-02* (2002), HCI 065
[46] Mary Morgan, Director of Public Information, House of Lords, in evidence to the Commission
[47] House of Commons Commission, *Twenty-Fourth Annual Report 2001-2002* (The Stationery Office; London 2002)

3.23 These recent statements on accessibility and communication are welcome and are leading to improvements, some of which we discuss in the next chapter. But they do not amount to a strategy.

3.24 A strategy should provide:
- focus and momentum for change
- a comprehensive agenda which tackles all aspects of the issue
- an agreed set of ambitions against which people and institutions can be held to account, together with appropriate measures and criteria
- processes to achieve targets, including clear responsibilities both for the overall programme and for specific tasks
- a process also for involving and engaging those with responsibility and interest in the outcome
- and the necessary resources to secure its goals.

3.25 A strategy needs to cover a number of years and be consulted upon among MPs and Peers, media and public. There need to be annual targets and a process of evaluation which incorporates independent elements.

3.26 Corporate goals and indicative measures relating to communication are to be found in the House of Commons Commission Annual Report.[48] While recent developments in both Houses reflect a desire for a more strategic approach to communication, they do not amount to a strategy with the characteristics listed above. For a start there was little or no consultation in the planning of these 'strategies' – most MPs and Peers seem unaware of them; there seems similarly to have been little or no discussion with the media or public, let alone with those communities which evidence suggests are most alienated from parliamentary processes. Nor are there any of the timetables, responsibilities, budgetary commitments or review processes of a strategy that can honestly be said to be worth the name. There is no document which sets out a strategy looking comprehensively at all aspects of Parliament's interaction with the public, beginning with an assessment of what the public need and have a right to expect from their Parliament.

3.27 This Report in its recommendations contains many of the objectives we think a parliamentary communication strategy should adopt. It is not our role to draw up a detailed strategy for both Houses, but we would again assert the need for the strategy to be based on the principles set out in this Report.

---

[48] Annual reports of the House of Commons Commission can be found at www.publications.parliament.uk/pa/cm/cmhocpap.htm

3.28 **We recommend a communication strategy for Parliament which is arrived at through a wide-reaching and open process of consultation with parliamentarians, the media, the public and other interested bodies.**

3.29 **The communication strategy should take Parliament at least to 2010 with provision for a mid-term review, and it should be based on the optimum principles we have outlined – accessibility and transparency; participation and responsiveness; accountability; inclusiveness; best practice in management and communication.**

3.30 **Once drafted by the parliamentary authorities, the communication strategy should be tabled for agreement by both Houses.**

3.31 **The communication strategy will require regular reporting back to MPs and Peers, annual evaluation against targets, and provision for the public to participate in the evaluation process.**

Budget

3.32 A comprehensive and effective communication strategy for Parliament will cost money. There is currently no identifiable communications budget for Parliament. Items of communication are subsumed within general departmental budgets. Moreover, there appears to be a commitment overall not to increase Parliament's budget from 2001-02 levels, with only some provision for modest growth beyond the medium term – mainly for investment in technology and to meet unforeseen requirements. This is incompatible with Parliament's need to dramatically improve its communication with the public.

3.33 Parliament's expenditure on communication is hard to estimate given that Parliament's communication effort is so decentralised. An approximate estimate provided to us by GIP, excluding visitor arrangements but including other major elements of communication, is between £2 million and £2.5 million for staffing and other direct costs such as publications designed for the public (but not, for example, *Hansard* or select committee reports). When overheads such as accommodation and telecommunications are taken into account, a further £1.5 million should be added to the costing. About 31 staff are directly employed in communication areas.

3.34 Of course a comparison with Government is not comparing like with like, but it is worth noting that the Phillis Review in 2004 estimated that some 2,600 people worked in Government communications directorates and that the total cost of advertising, marketing and other paid-for publicity, as well as staff costs, was around £320 million.[49] The purpose of such communication is vastly different from that of Parliament but it gives some sense of scale to Parliament's current communication efforts. Parliament's current expenditure is not meeting its communication needs nor has it kept pace with expenditure in the outside world. In what is increasingly characterised as a media and communications age, Government and corporate resourcing of communication has increased dramatically.

3.35 MORI research undertaken for the Hansard Society showed that members of the public, when made aware that future communication initiatives could be costly, generally viewed expenditure on information about Parliament as a reasonable use of public funds.[50]

3.36 Democracy is a public good worth investing in. The communication strategy should in the first instance be determined by what the public have a right to expect of a modern Parliament. The resulting costs can then be debated publicly as part of the process of agreeing the strategy. There will be a significant cost to re-engaging the public and Parliament should not be embarrassed by that fact. For a sum equivalent to a single lottery roll-over, Parliament's communication with the public could be radically transformed.

3.37 **The communication strategy must be accompanied by the necessary and long-term budgetary commitment from the parliamentary authorities.**

Our recommendations

R1 A Communications Service should be established for Parliament, bringing together within its departmental remit the various communication activities essential to a contemporary democratic institution

R2 A single Joint Committee of both Houses should be established, responsible for communication matters, though MPs or Peers should be able to consider separately matters solely relevant to their respective Houses

R3 A communication strategy for Parliament should be adopted, having been arrived at through a wide-reaching and open process of consultation with parliamentarians, the media, the public and other interested bodies

---

[49] Phillis, B. et al., *An Independent Review of Government Communications* (Cabinet Office; London 2004)
[50] MORI, *Enhancing Engagement* (2004)

R4 The communication strategy should take Parliament at least to 2010 with provision for a mid-term review, and it should be based on the optimum principles of accessibility and transparency; participation and responsiveness; accountability; inclusiveness; and best practice in management and communication

R5 The communication strategy should be tabled for agreement by both Houses

R6 The communication strategy will require regular reporting back to MPs and Peers, annual evaluation against targets, and provision for the public to participate in the evaluation process

R7 The communication strategy must be accompanied by the necessary and long-term budgetary commitment from the parliamentary authorities.

CHAPTER 4

ELEMENTS OF A COMMUNICATION STRATEGY

CHAPTER FOUR
Elements of a communication strategy

A communication strategy for Parliament should address all those routes through which the public deal with Parliament – the media, the internet, the classroom and community, and in visits to Parliament.

The strategy should forge a better relationship between Parliament and the media in order to improve coverage for the public; provide a radically enhanced website to allow real involvement in Parliament's work from all sections of society; increase the resources, facilities and opportunities for engagement by young people; encourage a review of how Parliament goes about its work to re-engage the public with Parliament's functions.

When fully and consistently applied, the principles of communication outlined in this Report should have an effect at every level of parliamentary life – always placing the emphasis on the rights and interests of the public.

4.1 We have made clear that for Parliament to re-engage with the public, it can no longer be a place which is seen to involve people only once every four or five years at the ballot box. A new relationship must be forged between Parliament and the public in which people feel continually involved and listened to. Parliament must become more 'us' and less 'them'. A Communications Department, a communication strategy, a communication budget – these basic elements of successful engagement, commonplace elsewhere in public and commercial life, should, as a matter of urgency, be adopted by Parliament.

4.2 The process of drafting a detailed communication strategy is for Parliament to own and complete. We have set out above what we see to be the prerequisites for this process – for consultation, agreement, review and resourcing. In this chapter we look at some of the necessary elements of a successful communication strategy. Such a strategy would enhance the functions of Parliament, namely: the scrutiny of Government policies and actions; representing and communicating the views and interests of constituents; and debating, approving, amending or rejecting, as appropriate, proposed legislation.

4.3 The public can come across Parliament in a number of ways: in the media, on the internet, in the classroom and community, on visits to Parliament itself. In all these areas Parliament has made a number of changes and improvements, some of which we outline below. We welcome all such progress. An understanding within Parliament of the necessity for effective communication is gradually emerging. The recent report from the Modernisation Committee, *Connecting Parliament with the Public*, was a particularly important contribution.[51] But the scope of such change has been limited by a lack of clear political leadership, a lack of comprehensive reform, a lack of strategic vision, and endemic weaknesses in Parliament as an organisation. We hope that the recommendations of our Report will provide the required momentum for parliamentarians and officials alike to catch up and keep pace with the society around them.

Improving media coverage

4.4 Research shows that trust and respect for an institution increase as knowledge and understanding of that institution is strengthened. It follows that the more information that reaches the public about Parliament, the better. In this section we examine the steps Parliament can take to improve the amount and quality of its media coverage.

Copyright Telegraph Group Limited (late 1960s)

4.5 As noted in Chapter Two, it would be a mistake in this context to mourn the passing of some 'golden age' of parliamentary reporting. It is certainly true that the press used to devote more column inches to the activities of Parliament, but it is easy to confuse quantity with quality and to exaggerate the impact such coverage ever had upon readers. The question, in any case, is not how we should restore old practices, for that is neither feasible nor desirable. The question is how Parliament should set out its stall in the age of 24/7 electronic media, unprecedented competition among newspapers and the exciting opportunities offered by the new media. As we have said before, our recommendations are emphatically not governed by nostalgia, but by a desire to see Parliament adapt itself to fit the needs and pressures of the modern world.

---

[51] House of Commons Select Committee on Modernisation of the House of Commons, *Connecting Parliament with the Public: First Report of Session 2003-04* (2004), HC 368

4.6 Parliament must reassess its relationship with the media in light of the core principles of accessibility, transparency and accountability. Both in written submissions and in the seminars we held with media representatives we repeatedly heard the complaint that a culture of mutual suspicion had arisen between Parliament and journalists. Reporters feel they are automatically viewed as potential trouble-makers or even the 'enemy' by the parliamentary authorities – self-evidently, a perception which makes effective parliamentary communication all but impossible. While it is inevitable that journalists will often find themselves in an adversarial relationship with individual politicians or parties, there is no reason why the relationship between the press and Parliament *per se* should be hostile. Quite the opposite, in fact: the media and Parliament have an overwhelming shared interest in co-operation, which, if developed, could be to the great benefit of the public. There is a strong case for the formalisation of the relationship: **A new Communications Department should set up an advisory group of media representatives**.

Comments from the media:

Elinor Goodman, Political Editor of Channel 4 News, put it starkly when speaking to the Modernisation Committee: 'You are in a competitive news market where other people are trying to guide us and sell us stories. What you are selling us are essentially lists.'[52]

The Evening Standard called for '...a small unit with an official who is senior enough to use discretion about what is put out. A Press Office could also act as an interface with the Speaker and the Serjeant's office and with committee clerks who are usually helpful but understandably cautious in dealing with the Press.'[53]

The *Daily Mail* said, 'While an avalanche of paper is issued every day covering every aspect of what is happening in Parliament, the House authorities make little effort to make it digestible, accessible or relevant.'[54]

4.7 Parliament as an institution also needs the confidence to identify its own 'news' to communicate to the media. Hitherto, Parliament has tended to provide *information* but not news. It has been left to journalists to sift through the countless webpages and press releases for items of interest. A number of editors and journalists explicitly called upon Parliament to be more active in guiding reporters, without resorting to 'spin'.

---

[52] Select Committee on Modernisation, *Connecting Parliament with the Public* (2004)
[53] The *Evening Standard* in evidence to the Commission
[54] The *Daily Mail* in evidence to the Commission

4.8 In a frantic world of deadlines and limited time it is not surprising – as was admitted by many journalists who spoke to us – that good parliamentary stories are so often missed. It is also not surprising that the well-packaged Government story is more readily picked up. Parliament also has to accept that media organisations are much leaner than they used to be, and can no longer spare journalists to spend their time in the gallery or a committee room in the hope of coming across a story. Journalists pick up stories from their contacts, from official press officers and from one another, not from long hours sitting expectantly with a notepad in the gallery. These are the realities of the modern media, and Parliament has to adapt to them if its profile is to rise.

4.9 The parliamentary website's homepage should highlight significant proceedings about to take place, or the headline findings of select committee reports published that day. A cursory look at websites of the Scottish Parliament, the Australian House of Representatives and the London Assembly, to take just three examples, shows how our own Parliament could easily move to a more 'news-based' approach.

4.10 Traditionally, parliamentary officials have been reluctant to be involved in selection or editorialising of any kind. There are understandable concerns about appearing partisan, and offending political parties, Members or committees by what is highlighted and what is not. Even so, there is already recognition *within* Parliament of the need for change: the submission we received from the Clerk of the House of Commons and the Clerk of the Parliaments acknowledged that the website needed 'a more informative "news" page with daily changing content'.[55]

4.11 While some committees already receive good coverage for their work by virtue of controversial subjects, media-savvy chairs or inherent public interest, this is now being complemented by the work of select committee media officers. They are now choosing particular reports to push to media outlets and explaining why the findings are of particular news interest. Were they to treat every committee report and recommendation with equal weight their work would quickly be discredited. We accept that doing the same for legislative debates, for example, is a more sensitive matter as one of the advantages for officials of promoting select committee activity is its cross-party nature. But this problem need not be insuperable. When the media show interest in particular issues during the second reading of a specific bill, parliamentary officials would be completely justified in drawing

---

[55] Clerk of the House and Clerk of the Parliaments in evidence to the Commission

journalists' attention to relevant debates and amendments during standing committee and report stage. The subsequent increase in media attention to these stages of the legislative process might also improve the quality of MPs' detailed scrutiny of bills.

4.12 **We recommend that parliamentary officials do much more to draw the media's attention explicitly to matters of public interest.**

4.13 This should not be confused with the quite separate process of press briefing by political parties and individual MPs concerning parliamentary matters. Indeed, the whole point is that Parliament needs to provide an independent corrective to this, acting as a modern institution which alerts the media (and thus the public) to important proceedings in a clear and neutral way. Parliamentary officials need the confidence to see that this is entirely consistent with their traditions of neutrality. MPs need to accept that communication of this sort is not inherently partisan.

4.14 In embracing openness more enthusiastically, Parliament must also reconsider seemingly arbitrary restrictions on reporting which still exist. Journalists and broadcasters told the Commission of their longstanding concerns that Parliament imposes unnecessary barriers to legitimate reporting. In particular, broadcasters criticised the current rules of broadcasting in the chambers and elsewhere in the parliamentary precincts as being far too restrictive.

4.15 Channel Five told the Commission that, 'Another reason why Five News, in common with other news programmes, has reduced its coverage of Parlia-

Copyright Daily Express

"In order to restore the popularity ratings and the dignity of Parliament, I have introduced some new talent to the Commons..."

ment is because of the severe restrictions which apply to television news organisations. In particular, the largely static TV coverage within the chambers and the limited access for cameras within the precincts of Parliament.'[56] This opinion was shared by the BBC as well as other broadcasters.

---

[56] Channel Five in evidence to the Commission

4. Elements of a communication strategy

4.16 Removing unnecessary restrictions would not only make possible more and higher quality coverage, but would also be a powerful symbol of Parliament's institutional desire to improve its openness and responsiveness to the public, and its recognition that the institution belongs to the nation, not only to those who work or are elected to serve there. When providing evidence to the Commission, Channel 4 said that, 'In return for giving up some of their privacy, we believe that parliamentarians would be giving out an important message to viewers – "This is your building. We are your representatives." The feeling given off at the moment is that the building belongs to MPs and Lords – not to the people.'[58]

4.17 The current rules for broadcast coverage of parliamentary proceedings are determined by the Broadcasting Committee,

One of the longest sittings of Parliament took place in March 2005 when the Anti-Terror Bill went back and forth between the House of Commons and House of Lords. The BBC's Political Editor, Andrew Marr, subsequently wrote that when Parliament's broadcasting rules are unnecessarily restrictive it is the public who miss out:

'Parliament is so important and yet so television-hostile that even I despair. The truth about last week's marathon sitting of both Houses is that it was a great democratic achievement this country could be proud of.

'Television viewers were cheated of perhaps the best demonstration of parliamentary democracy doing what it should that there has been for decades. Thanks to the rules Parliament imposes, voters could not see it happening, or gain any real visual sense of the struggle. We cannot show reaction shots, or cut around the chambers in a way that gives a sense of rhetorical drama. Nor can we film anywhere else, except in the central Lobby, and even then under severe restrictions

'I had wanted to show, for instance, the sterling efforts of the catering staff, working round the clock serving up fried breakfasts, coffee and sustaining meals. But no . . . It would have been wonderful to show the voting lobbies, crowded in the small hours with famous faces; or to be invited into the morale-boosting meetings of either side; or to interview weary, defiant parliamentarians on the Commons terrace; or even to talk to the tough, seen-it-all, rather shrewd staff of the two Houses. But all this is forbidden, and I cannot understand why.

'We live in a television-saturated age and in a parliamentary democracy which is not as noticed as it needs to be. And these two facts are somehow connected.'[57]

---

[57] Andrew Marr writing in the *Daily Telegraph*, 16 March 2005
[58] Channel 4 in evidence to the Commission

the most recent version of the rules being found as an Annex to their First Report of Session 2002-03, *The Rules of Coverage*.[59] We will not rehearse all details of the rules but two recent examples of their application give a flavour of their effect and implementation. When purple paint was thrown at the Prime Minister during Prime Minister's Questions in May 2004, the BBC showed a slow-motion shot of the paint landing on the frontbench. Otherwise the incident would have been so quick as to be invisible. When supporters of fox hunting entered the chamber from behind the Speaker's Chair in September 2004, the wide-angle shot of the chamber was used to show how access was achieved. In both cases, although the BBC felt there was a clear public interest in showing what took place, it was severely reprimanded by the parliamentary authorities: slow-motion shots are forbidden as is the use of the wide-angle shot of the end of the chamber for anything other than editing purposes.

4.18 Of course, such restrictions do not only have an impact on coverage of (comparatively rare) instances of disorder. The tight rules governing close-ups and reaction shots, for example, are felt by broadcasters to result in static and unengaging television. The Broadcasting Committee also considered such representations in its Report. The Committee heard the same appeals as this Commission from the BBC and Channel 4 for relaxation of coverage rules. In the Committee's findings, the successful experience in Scotland of shots of the public gallery and of cutaways is cited – only then to be unaccountably rejected. The Committee argues that only a single feed without cutaways and other variations can meet the different requirements of the various broadcasters. We do not believe this to be a valid argument. All broadcasters seem to be united in favour of these changes and are used to ironing out such different expectations in a responsible manner through discussion.

4.19 The refusal to relax the rules of coverage in response to the requests of broadcasters is just another example of decisions being made about Parliament's communication on an ad hoc basis, without a proper strategy and agreed set of principles. The Committee states the objective of broadcasting to be the provision of 'a full, balanced, fair and accurate account of proceedings, with the aim of informing viewers about the work of the House'. In doing this, the director should 'have regard to the dignity of the House and to its function as a working body rather than a place of entertainment'. We agree with these objectives, but their interpretation by

---

[59] House of Commons Broadcasting Select Committee, *The Rules of Coverage* (2003), HC 786

MPs seems to ignore the advice of experts about modern communication and how it works. There is no attempt to define what 'added value' the televising of Parliament brings to the work of *Hansard*. Reforming the rules on broadcasting would provide real accessibility and transparency for the public, rather than merely a visual record of contributions in the chambers.

4.20 **We recommend that the rules of television coverage in the chambers be relaxed to allow, for example, appropriate reaction shots, the relevant use of close-ups, more panning shots of the backbenches and a greater range of coverage during divisions. It should be an explicit objective of parliamentary coverage to not just inform but to interest and engage the viewer.**

4.21 As previously noted, while rules for coverage of formal parliamentary proceedings are decided by the Broadcasting Committee, rules for filming elsewhere in the parliamentary estate are decided by the Administration Committee. Interview points have been agreed, one in Central Lobby, one in the Committee Corridor outside Committee Room 16 (the Committee later stopped any filming at this point relating to meetings of the Parliamentary parties), one on the first floor of Portcullis House and one in the atrium of Portcullis House. Walking shots are not allowed in corridors. Interviews can only take place with Members and even then only 'on a parliamentary subject'.

4.22 While any improvements in access are welcome, it is the Central Lobby point which is mostly used. This is perhaps in part a result of the restrictive rules being applied. The Committee work in the Committee Corridor and Portcullis House would come alive from the broadcasters' point of view if, in addition to Members, they could interview witnesses or attending members of the public. Walking shots, with the agreement of the Member concerned, are an obvious means of enlivening coverage. But the BBC was reprimanded for showing the Prime Minister walking to a crucial Parliamentary Labour Party meeting, jacket over shoulder and shirtsleeves rolled up. Restricting those issues which may be discussed to 'a parliamentary subject' also unnecessarily limits the public's sense of what goes on in Parliament to overtly formal proceedings. The work of all-party groups or particular events held in Parliament are of wide interest to the public and should also be accessible to film crews.

4.23 There is an understandable concern that film crews do not interfere, or obstruct those in Parliament going about their daily work, or film individuals without their consent. However, **we recommend relaxation of the rules for filming in** the precincts of Parliament, permission for walking shots, interviews with relevant persons other than MPs, and a wider interpretation of parliamentary subject-matter which genuinely reflects the richness of political activity taking place at any one time within Parliament.

4.24 It is not only broadcasters who are affected by the existing restrictions. Newspapers are effectively prevented from using still photographs from the chamber on their front pages. *The Guardian* told the Commission that Westminster's ban on access to still photographs is a real block to their work.[60] **We recommend that the ban on still photographs should be reconsidered in light of the communication principles set out above.**

4.25 An increased number of journalist passes need to be issued to reflect the extraordinary expansion of the media. At present web-based journalists, subject-specialist journalists and others told us that they find it difficult to obtain passes and thus access to the precincts. If Parliament wants more coverage and less of the 'Westminster village' mentality to dominate the way it is reported, it is clearly in the institution's interest to open its doors to those outside the traditional group of broadcasters and newspapers.

4.26 There are obvious implications in increased access of this kind, not least for security and facilities, but in a modern democracy we do not believe that these can be allowed to remain insurmountable. They are certainly outweighed by the prospective benefits to media and Parliament alike. This is not about office space, but about access. Again, to go back to our core principles, we should start from the proposition that Parliament needs a good reason to deny a parliamentary pass to a properly accredited journalist who can make a reasonable case for regular access. There should be a presumption of access, not a presumption of exclusion. **We recommend that the current restrictions on the number of passes available for media outlets be reconsidered.**

4.27 It amazed us how many seasoned reporters still admitted to difficulties finding their way round parliamentary documents and information. An induction process could be a way of opening up Parliament to media contacts, and of strengthening working relationships between parliamentary staff and journalists. **We recommend that the parliamentary authorities provide regular, formal induction for journalists.**

---

[60] *The Guardian* in evidence to the Commission

4. Elements of a communication strategy

The internet

4.28 We have emphasised the need for a fundamental rethink by Parliament of its relationship to the citizen, in which the principle of encouraging participation will be an essential component. Interactive, digital technologies provide a timely and fast-developing opportunity to expand and enrich public participation in Parliament's work.

4.29 The need to reform the website was a constant theme in the evidence we received. We were told by the parliamentary administration that some changes have been recently introduced through a redesign in July 2002 and others are planned. They concede that, 'The site still meets the needs of the specialist user more effectively than those of the casual visitor'[61] – for 'casual visitor' we would have written 'members of the public'. The recent report of the Modernisation Committee, *Connecting Parliament with the Public*, has called for 'a radical upgrading of the website at an early opportunity, which will require significant investment in systems and staff'.[62] We agree wholeheartedly with this assessment.

4.30 As we investigated this issue it became apparent that there is no clear governance of the website within Parliament – various officials are involved via an e-group in the House of Lords and a web group in the House of Commons but there is no strategic or overall authority and control. If one year's radical redesign is not to become the following year's out-of-date embarrassment there must be continuous consultation and improvement. **We recommend that a new Communications Department establish effective processes to manage, edit, develop and continually update the parliamentary website**.

4.31 The site remains in essence an online archival resource, impenetrable to most people, difficult to navigate, with almost no opportunity for interaction, and a wholly inadequate search engine. We have found commercial search engines such as Google immeasurably superior to Parliament's own search engine in finding material on the parliamentary site. There are few photographs and hardly any effective visual content, the overall impression being dry and thoroughly unengaging.

4.32 The gap between Parliament's website and those of many private companies, and indeed parts of Whitehall, is massive. Other outlets are providing resources that should be covered by the parliamentary website, for example

---

[61] Roger Sands, Clerk of the House, and Paul Hayter, Clerk of the Parliaments, in evidence to the Commission
[62] Select Committee on Modernisation, *Connecting Parliament with the Public* (2004), para 50

the faxyourmp.com and theyworkforyou.com websites. Such websites give valuable detail on the voting record of individual MPs and provide issues-based searches and email alerts. Parliament is failing to provide a badly needed democratic service.

4.33 In the wider world, many are contributing to discussion boards, blogs, wikis, email lists, texting, sms exchanges, but you would not know it from a visit to the parliamentary site. We are not advocating these developments for their own sake, and not all developments will always be appropriate for Parliament, but increasingly the public, and in particular teenagers and young adults, will expect such provision from any organisation which claims to be responsive let alone represent them in the wider world.

4.34 The House of Commons Commission's response to the Modernisation Committee's website recommendation states that 'more extensive changes are being planned for as part of the second phase of the Parliamentary Information Management Services (PIMS) project and the third phase of the Web Centre project. A business case will be prepared for the development of external access to PIMS, which would then become the primary means of providing public access to parliamentary information.'[63]

4.35 The public have a right to a clear commitment from the parliamentary authorities to modern internet accessibility. Used creatively, digital media could communicate Parliament more directly to citizens. We propose below five ways in which this could happen.

4.36 **Information on demand:** Citizens leading busy lives want to access information at their own convenience. Webcasts of debates and committee meetings should be archived and there should be a simple search facility enabling citizens to find *Hansard* reports, documents and webcasts by issue or the name of a particular MP. There should be links from archived material to relevant online consultative and discussion fora on the parliamentary website, enabling a constant interflow between the parliamentary output of information and citizens' input of comments and experience.

4.37 **Personalised information:** A key characteristic of new media is the capacity to narrowcast: whereas broadcasters try to talk to 'everyone', the internet can be used to target smaller communities and even individuals. Parliament should move towards providing personalised information on demand to

---

[63] House of Commons Commission, *Connecting Parliament with the Public: the House of Commons Commission's Response to the Committee's First Session of 2003-2004* (2004), HC 69, p 4

those who want it. Email and sms alerts to those with an interest in particular issues and policies – or the activities of their own MP – should be provided. One member of our Citizens' Panel argued, 'If we are to use the "new" technology to gain accessibility then the real issue is to ensure people get to find out about what they are interested in and what affects them. So for me the key is to do with segmentation and registration of the various audiences and populations.'[64] Another participant in our Panel asked, 'Who has time to dredge through all the reports? I don't. What I need is to be able to register with a service which can alert me to the dates and times of specific debates or committees, so that I can either follow them on TV or radio, or read a summarised report, without bias or sensationalism.'[65]

4.38 Parliament recently introduced an email alert system and this is to be welcomed. It is not well presented and there is only a very basic ability to customise alerts. It is nevertheless an important basis from which to develop a more sensitive system which could, for example, be customised according to the parliamentary activities of your local MP or issues of interest.

4.39 **Interactivity:** An important feature of digital ICT is the possibility of feedback. Broadcasting is defined by one-to-many transmission. The internet allows people to talk back. A website saying, 'This is who we are, but we're not particularly interested in who you are' does not fit with the culture of the internet. One of the most successful uses of the internet by parliamentarians has been online consultations with members of the public who can offer knowledge or experience relevant to particular areas of policy or legislation. The Modernisation Committee has stated that, 'We believe that the greater use of online consultation is a good way for Parliament to take account of the views of the wider public.'[66] In his study of two of the online parliamentary consultations, Stephen Coleman concluded that, 'Most

> *Feedback from the Commission's own Citizens' Panel included the following comments:*
>
> 'It's the first time I have ever taken part in anything remotely political and I enjoyed it immensely … Not sure how relevant my comments were, as I'm not particularly educated or a "political animal" but I felt comfortable enough to take part.'
>
> 'I would like to thank you for the opportunity to take part in this exercise. If anything, I feel less disenfranchised for having taken part.'

---

[64] Comment from member of the Commission's Citizens' Panel
[65] Comment from member of the Commission's Citizens' Panel
[66] Select Committee on Modernisation, *Connecting Parliament with the Public* (2004), para 53

participants in both of the consultations were not 'the usual suspects': party members, lobbyists or people who lived in or around the Westminster village. The voices heard in these consultation forums would probably not otherwise have been heard by parliamentarians.'[67]

4.40 **Peer-to-peer:** As well as traditionally 'vertical' paths of one-to-many and many-to-one communication, the internet is facilitating new, dispersed networks of peer-to-peer interaction. Many of these groups have a direct interest in linking with the work of Parliament. For example, an online network such as Netmums, in which mothers with toddlers share information, experiences and opinions, could be linked in to select committee inquiries where issues affecting parents of small children are being considered. The point here is that parliamentary communication is not just a matter of enabling 'outsiders' to see what is going on in Parliament, but also about using communication technology to make possible dramatically better models of 'knowledge exchange' between the work of Parliament and wider social networks.

4.41 **Connecting institutions:** As governance becomes more devolved, citizens need to communicate with a range of different institutions that represent them – and representatives in such institutions need to exchange views with one another. The easy links made possible via the web should be used to ensure that different levels of representation are obvious to citizens, and accessible through a single front door, and that elected representatives can interact together in one online space.

4.42 We must also mention the potential of individual MPs' websites to communicate effectively something of Parliament's work. While, as we explained at the outset of this Report, communication by individual MPs to their constituents has not been the focus of our inquiry, we must acknowledge the good work in this area done by an increasing number of MPs.

4.43 **We recommend that the parliamentary website be radically improved. In doing so, the following requirements should be met:**

- **It should be proactive as well as reactive – the purpose of the site should not be simply to provide information to those already in the know, but should invite participation from people who are not familiar with the workings of Parliament**

---

[67] Coleman, S., 'Connecting Parliament to the Public via the Internet: Two case studies of online consultations' in *Information, Communication & Society* Vol 7, No 1 (March 2004), pp 1-22

- **Visits to the website should enable citizens to become engaged through contributing, where appropriate, to interactive discussions and consultations**
- **Attempts should be made to provide more than one level of access to material, with the availability of explanatory summaries provided as well as original documents**
- **The site should provide constantly updated information about the parliamentary schedule**
- **Parliament should work to integrate the interactive features of the web with the live coverage of proceedings on BBC Parliament**
- **The site should meet accessibility requirements. It needs to be easily navigable and searchable by, for example, topic and MP. A site with a low bandwidth would better suit those without broadband access.**

4.44 Research by the Hansard Society has found that, at present, most people are unaware of the parliamentary website.[68] **An improved website should engage the widest range of citizens, using well-designed publicity and targeted advertising to help people understand that there is a virtual route through which they have easy access to their Parliament.**

Young people

'... they [young people] care far more about broad social issues than the narrow world of politics and politicians.'[69]

4.45 Young people have widely been identified as a group that is less engaged with traditional politics and Parliament. We argue that building connections with young people is central to Parliament's longer-term health and effectiveness. Whereas in the past people tended to vote in greater numbers as they grew older and took on the responsibilities of mortgage, job, family etc, it now appears that habits of not voting, of feeling

Copyright Hansard Society

Interviewing young people at Parliament

disengaged from the institutional political process, are continuing and even

---

[68] Hansard Society, *Connecting Communities with Parliament* (Hansard Society, 2004)
[69] Save the Children, *On the Right Track: What matters to young people in the UK?* (Save the Children; London 2003)

deepening as people enter their later 20s and 30s. The social and political trends we identify among young people today are not just signs of youth but are fast becoming aspects of adulthood.

4.46 Article 12 of the United Nations Convention on the Rights of the Child states that young people have a right to have their opinions heard when decisions are being made that will affect them. Government and the devolved executives have responded to this through the introduction of policy initiatives and greater opportunities for young people to be involved in consultations.[70] Parliament is once again lagging behind and needs to be more aware and responsive to the policies being put in place by other institutions. Many decisions made in Parliament affect young people and therefore they should have appropriate opportunities to feed into decision-making processes.

4.47 Members of our Young People's Working Group argued that young people are interested in political issues, but do not always understand Parliament's role in dealing with these issues. Many young people have little understanding of how our political system works and the dominant figures within it. Recent polling by ICM for Ofsted found that only 16 per cent of 14-16 year olds could recognise the leader of the main opposition party at the time.[71] These findings were mirrored in the experiences of a participant in the Commission's online Citizens' Panel, 'I'm an A-level student (of politics incidentally) but apart from in my politics lessons, the vacuum of even basic understanding is scary . . . young people now eligible to vote simply don't understand the system, let alone what the political parties stand for. Therein lies the problem with voter apathy . . . The fact is, with so much pressure of exams, social commitments, and the whole multitude of activities, duties and chores that young people are expected to carry out nowadays, what seem like minor concerns, such as politics, are simply left behind.'[72]

4.48 Parliament must not ignore nor isolate itself from the growing trend of young people's disengagement with and ignorance of parliamentary politics. Parliament still has the opportunity to re-engage young people – and continue this relationship throughout their lives. If Parliament fails to communicate with young people it is denying itself a future.

---

[70] This includes the DfES guidance found in *Pupil Participation Guidance: Working Together – Giving Children and Young People a Say* (DfES; London 2004). This recommends how children and young people can be involved in school management issues

[71] ICM, 'Citizenship Poll' (December 2004)

[72] Comment from member of the Commission's Citizens' Panel

4. Elements of a communication strategy

Citizenship education and participation in community issues

4.49 Citizenship education is a new and developing part of the school curriculum, and has been statutory in secondary schools in England since 2002; in Scotland it is now one of the five National Priorities for Education from primary school age; in Wales it is part of Personal and Social Education, and Northern Ireland is preparing to launch in 2006. Political Literacy features as a key element in each of the four nations, with emphasis on participation and skills development, as well as knowledge and understanding. Citizenship education is ambitious in its goals, and as stated by Sir Bernard Crick, a former adviser to the Home Office, in drawing up his recommendations for the English Curriculum:

> 'We aim at no less than a change in political culture in this country both nationally and locally ... to build on and extend radically to young people the best in existing traditions of community life and public service, and to make them individually confident in finding new forms of involvement and action among themselves.'[73]

4.50 **We recommend that Parliament considers its role in consistently developing citizenship education resources and the different curriculum approaches across the UK. It should work closely with other organisations to support more training for teachers, and more and better materials for young people.** The introduction of citizenship education in schools, as well as wider participation policies, provides Parliament with an historic opportunity to communicate its value to young people and involve them in its activities. Materials should be a mix of factual information on structures and process and, more importantly, information on specific issues and debates.

4.51 The British Youth Council (BYC) suggested to the Commission that it was vital for citizenship education to give young people real life experiences of how their democracy works. For example, in conjunction with other agencies, Parliament could link parliamentary activities such as debating and voting with school activity – be it mock elections, the work of school councils, or the study of particular local issues in which children discover how to engage constructively in political activity.

---

[73] Advisory Group on Citizenship, *Education for Citizenship and the Teaching of Democracy in Schools: the final report of the Advisory Group on Citizenship* (Qualifications and Curriculum Authority; London 1998)

4.52 We welcome recommendations made by the Modernisation Select Committee, which suggest that there should be a voter's pack for young people.[74] We would, however, stress that such initiatives should be planned in partnership with young people, through specialist advisory groups and a wider consultation process.

4.53 **We recommend that Parliament's facilities, including the chambers, should be made available during recess for groups of young people.** In the Scottish Parliament, the Presiding Officer has the power to allow young people to use the debating chamber.

4.54 **We recommend that Parliament takes young people, including pre-voting citizens, far more seriously by involving them in its processes and decision-making.** This must include integral and ongoing involvement in communication strategies and the Parliamentary Education Unit; consultation where relevant during select committee and pre-legislative committee inquiries; joint debates involving both parliamentarians and young people; the raising within Parliament (for example at select committee inquiries or Westminster Hall debates) of topics and issues brought to the attention of Members by young people (perhaps through UK Youth Parliament or school council recommendations); and regular e-updates on issues which young people can sign up to.

Visits to schools, further education colleges, training providers and youth organisations

4.55 Visits from parliamentarians to schools are important and are in need of development. There was agreement that regular visits by parliamentarians to institutions accessed by young people could enormously increase both understanding and interest in Parliament. We have noted the evidence that local MPs enjoy greater trust and respect than the institution of Parliament or MPs generally, so it seems sensible, to the greatest degree possible, to use the local MP as the ambassador for Parliament.

4.56 This is backed up by evidence, cited by The Electoral Commission, that young people value face-to-face contact and communication taking place in their own environments.[75] The Electoral Commission points to roadshows as a key way of communicating their messages, particularly to older young people and those who are not in school. We refer to Young Scot as an example of

---

[74] Select Committee on Modernisation, *Connecting Parliament with the Public* (2004), Recommendation 10
[75] The Electoral Commission in evidence to the Commission

good practice – who, in partnership with the Scottish Executive, have a touring satellite van which runs sessions on topics relevant to young people.[76]

4.57 Despite considerable potential from such visits, there is currently little overall strategy as to how they should best take place; and little imagination given to their content and quality. David Kerr, of the National Foundation for Educational Research, told the Commission that there are 'very mixed responses' to MPs' visits.[77] Indeed, one girl told us: 'My only contact with anything to do with Parliament was when an MP came into school last week. He talked *at* us for half an hour and then when he was asked questions, he did not really answer them. I'm pretty interested in politics, but unfortunately there were no other words for it – he was just *boring!*'[78] Sir Bernard Crick thought that the quality of MPs' visits could be significantly improved, and linked to debates in Parliament, aspects of the citizenship curriculum and other processes of participation and involvement.[79]

The Parliamentary Education Unit and community outreach

4.58 We have already mentioned the Parliamentary Education Unit and its work. The PEU is at the heart of Parliament's current strategy for communicating with young people. The PEU works on behalf of both Houses of Parliament and provides 'resources and support for teachers and students to increase their knowledge and understanding of the role, work and history of Parliament'.[80] The PEU currently has five full-time and one part-time members of staff.

Australia: The Parliamentary Education Office in Australia has been delivering role-play programmes in Parliament House for over 10 years. Each year they deliver the programmes to approximately 79,000 students. Participants can experience a little bit of what it means to be a federal parliamentarian, complete with sets and props.

The Parliamentary Education Office has professional development programmes for teachers. In one such programme, Parliamentary Education Fellows are immersed in Parliament for a week and then go home to create programmes in their own communities. These can vary from one-off conventions to on-going, home-grown programmes.

---

[76] Young Scot provides information for 12-26 year-olds in Scotland. It offers incentives, information and opportunities to help young people in Scotland make informed choices and play a part in their community
[77] David Kerr in evidence to the Commission
[78] Evidence to the Commission
[79] Sir Bernard Crick in evidence to the Commission
[80] Clerk of the House of Commons and Clerk of the Parliaments in evidence to the Commission

4.59 Among its resources is an education website, Explore Parliament, at www.explore.parliament.uk, which contains materials for teachers, including lesson plans linked to the national curriculum, and information, games and activities for young people. Website material and print material need to be expanded from educational documentation about parliamentary processes and language to topical features on parliamentary news and developments, and issues-based material which can be more readily deployed in the wider process of citizenship education. The Explore Parliament website must compete with online educational material available elsewhere, such as the BBC Citizen X website. It should provide opportunities for young people's participation and focus more on current issues and interactivity. In addition, the website currently attempts to cater for 5-18 year-olds. This is too wide a remit; the website should have specific age-group sections.

4.60 The PEU also provides publications aimed at students of different ages, two videos explaining Parliament, one for students aged 14-18 and one for those aged 8-13. The PEU organises a variety of visit programmes – 'although capacity is limited' – which include a series of 'pupil parliaments'. Staff are also available to give advice to teachers and students by email, post or phone.

4.61 The budget and number of staff necessary to train, communicate, prepare website and documentary material goes far beyond what is currently available. We have set out an agenda for connecting younger people with Parliament which must be incorporated into Parliament's communication strategy and be properly resourced. **In line with recent joint recommendations from the Accommodation and Works Committee and Administration Committee, we recommend that the PEU should have a well resourced and dedicated teaching space with multi-media facilities.**

4.62 **We recommend that Parliament employs more full-time and contracted staff who are fully trained and experienced in working with young people in a range of different settings.** In addition, young people need to be integrated into the internal decision-making of Parliament. As Parliament considers its websites, communication strategies, and visitor facilities, it needs to work with young people who can be involved in its decision-making and bring their perspectives to bear. **We recommend that a young persons' consultative group be established with the right to attend and advise at key administrative meetings of both Houses.**

4.63 **We recommend that more is done to enhance the effectiveness of parliamentary outreach work, with greater understanding of the needs of young people at different ages, and in different settings such** as pupil referral units or post-16 training centres. Training for MPs, Peers and parliamentary officials to manage the different needs of young people should be both available and encouraged. Such training would be carried out by experts whether in-house or employed by the PEU on a consultancy basis, and should also involve participation by young people. The PEU should progress beyond its current limited capacity and place a greater emphasis on outreach work.

4.64 The PEU should have a specified outreach role that encompasses not only young people, but the community at large. The Scottish Parliament and National Assembly for Wales provide clear models of how this can be piloted. The PEU should be proactive in bringing Parliament to members of the public; it should have established networks across the country and regional co-ordinators based outside London.

The Scottish Parliament and National Assembly for Wales have piloted parliamentary outreach programmes:

The Scottish Parliament offers four main areas of outreach:

- *Education Outreach* includes sessions in schools, Outreach Teachers' Seminars and also seminars for School Librarians. They also work with young people's groups.

- *Community Outreach* offers information sessions about the work of the Scottish Parliament and ways to participate for community groups across Scotland. Local MSPs are invited to attend the sessions and answer questions on both local and national issues.

- The *Voluntary Sector* are served through joint sessions with Scottish Council for Voluntary Organisations covering how the Scottish Parliament works and how to lobby.

- *Gaelic Outreach* offers information and education sessions to community groups, schools, further and higher education.

The National Assembly for Wales set up a Regional Public Information Service in 2003 to develop local networks as part of the Assembly's commitment to reach all the people of Wales. The service covers the four regions of Wales and plays a crucial role in the promotion of Regional Committee meetings in each area. Each region has two Regional Public Information Co-ordinators who are based locally.

An exhibition hall in North Wales provides visitors with an opportunity to access the most up-to-date information on who's who, what's happening and how the Assembly works.

Visits to Parliament

'It came as no surprise to read your article on the treatment of women MPs. I took a group of sixth-form politics students last year and was horrified to hear one of the tour guides openly express the view that the status and standing of Parliament had declined since more women were "allowed" in.

'Happily, both male and female students were also horrified by these views and so perhaps offer some hope that the next generation of parliamentarians will be more enlightened. Assuming, that is, women have not been put off entirely from the place.'[81]

4.65 Visits to Parliament will only ever be a small part of a wider communication strategy – too few can attend. But it does communicate an impression which is then passed on to others. Welcome attempts are being made at the moment to develop and modernise the tour of Parliament. There have been improvements to signage, refreshment facilities, disabled access, approval for a visitors' reception centre and, importantly, the creation of a Central Tours Office 'to streamline booking arrangements and tour provision'.

4.66 From the visits made by Commissioners and their advisers and from comments gathered from many members of the public it is clear that the visits are at present mainly a heritage tour. We have heard a number of anecdotes of guides admitting their ignorance of the current work of Parliament, never mind more inane comments such as the one cited in the letter above.

The National Assembly for Wales has an interactive learning centre at the Pierhead. It is equipped with multi media activities designed to teach young people about democracy and the National Assembly for Wales. All activities are linked to the National Curriculum. Pupils and students can:

• debate and vote in the mock chamber;

• visit the chamber;

• use touchscreens, web pages and video wall to complete the exhibition challenge;

• question an Assembly Member; and

• take part in workshops.

4.67 We believe the Central Tours Office must ensure visits are not just heritage tours for tourists but educational and engagement opportunities for citizens. The development of such tours must be done in conjunction with the PEU. With the establishment of a Communications Department and a communication strategy we would expect to see a clear statement of the

---

[81] Letter to *The Guardian* 8 December 2004

objectives of parliamentary visits, targets in terms of increased understanding and engagement, not simply throughput and general 'satisfaction', and the integration of parliamentary visits into the wider educational and communication work of Parliament. There should also be consideration of extending the route to take in, if only during recesses, a view of Portcullis House with its very different, contemporary atmosphere.

4.68 The Joint Report of the Commons Accommodation and Works and Administration Committees set out a range of desirable visitor facilities in addition to the visitors' reception centre,

Copyright Houses of Parliament

including an exhibition space, an educational facility, a ticket office for tours and bookshop/retail facility.[82] For the democratic potential of visits to be fully exploited we would strongly support the extension of visitor and educational facilities as proposed by the two domestic committees.

Making Parliament understandable

4.69 Our evidence showed how alienating much of Parliament's style and self-presentation are to the public. Any attempt at re-engagement with the public must address this problem. Parliamentary language is often obscure and confusing, reinforcing the view that Parliament is relevant only to a bygone age. Much is made of occasions when Parliament modernises a single term, such as 'Strangers'. On this basis it will take centuries to modernise all of Parliament's terminology and vocabulary. While occasional parliamentary ceremonies can

Comments from Citizens' Panel:

- 'While of course it is necessary to preserve the dignity of the institution, surely some of the practices and language could be brought into the 21st century?'

- 'My image of Parliament is of a primary school playground when full, and for the majority of the time a desolate scene of a handful of individuals spouting uninteresting tosh to a non-audience.'

- 'The only way to really engage the less academic people is to explain things in plain English. For example, with news programmes people tend to switch off when it comes to Parliament; it is not clear what exactly is happening due to the language and complexity.'

[82] Accommodation & Works and Administration Committees First Joint Report, *Visitor Facilities: Access to Parliament* (2004), HC 324

retain archaisms with no harm done, this is not the case for Parliament's day-to-day work. **We recommend a thorough review of the language and terminology Parliament uses in accordance with the communication principles set out above.** There is now considerable expertise on the implementation of plain English which could be usefully applied to Parliament.

4.70 Channel 4 told us, 'The language and procedures of Westminster are felt by many viewers to be arcane, over-complex and mystifying. Language and procedures that are simpler and more transparent would assist audiences in believing that politicians are accountable to the electorate and connected to the real world.'[83]

4.71 There should also be a critical look at Parliament's 'culture'. We are not going to make detailed recommendations for every eventuality but such issues as behaviour (even sleeping) in the chamber and reports of sexism all make lasting impressions on voters. We do not want to overstress such presentational points but these type of concerns were repeatedly expressed by our online panellists and in other similar surveys.

Where Parliament happens

4.72 The building itself communicates powerfully to the public before any MP stands up to speak. Our discussions revealed how many were struck by the different political cultures generated simply by the walk between the 'Palace' and Portcullis House. Online panellists were forthright – 'If Parliament were a private corporation it would have long ago left the Palace of Westminster and relocated to a building that suits its current activity – including the provision of a warm welcome and proper facilities to people who want to visit and engage with it. The grandeur and gold leaf is best left to the tourists. The working parts of Parliament should be more accessible, but we're talking about one of the world's most famous and important buildings. Increasingly these two things are at odds with each other.'[84]

Copyright Hansard Society

Public attend a meeting in Parliament

Comment from Citizens' Panel:

'Why not take Parliament on the road – look how successful the touring of "home grounds" has been for the England football team – why not take some parliamentary debates out beyond the confines of Westminster?'[85]

[83] Channel 4 in evidence to the Commission
[84] Comment from member of the Commission's Citizens' Panel
[85] Comment from member of the Commission's Citizens' Panel

4.73 It is important not to limit Parliament in the eyes of the public only to one heritage site. The Palace of Westminster will no doubt remain central to Parliament's work for many years to come but **we recommend that Parliament should hold more meetings outside London.**

4.74 **Select committees, for example, should hold more formal proceedings and public events beyond Westminster.** Although they frequently travel during inquiries, these visits are predominantly fact-finding and involve meeting experts and interest groups. We welcome such activity of course. But the advantage of formal proceedings and public meetings is that their work goes beyond information gathering to wider public engagement and participation. In evidence to the Commission, we were told that Parliament or particular committees should move around the country, in an effort to link into local communities and be seen to be engaged with the community rather than with a self-contained and self-regarding world of Parliament. A parliamentary presence throughout the UK would give reality to the principles of accessibility, participation and diversity.

Partner Library Networks: The Scottish Parliament set up a network of 80 Partner Libraries. These provide local communities with information from and about the Parliament. By working in close liaison with the Scottish Parliament's Public Information Service and Education Service, many enquiries can be dealt with through Partner Libraries. The network is the one of the most visible ways in which the Parliament delivers on its commitment to be open, accessible, accountable and participative.

Comments from Citizens' Panel:

- 'There should be a major overhaul of Parliamentary procedure, carried out not by long-serving Parliamentarians but by outsiders looking at the best examples from the UK, Commonwealth and other legislatures.'

- 'While every organisation inevitably has its own rules and ways of behaving, Parliament does seem to go out of its way to exceed everyone in this regard . . . Even when they try to "modernise" proceedings, the solution they devise seems designed to emphasise their otherness – remember the last election for the Speaker, or the fiasco over determining the best structure for the second Chamber?'

- 'Parliament has to become – or at least be seen to be – accessible. This probably means not just physical access. But the proceedings must be understandably relevant to Joe Public as well as Dr Josephus Publicus.'

Parliamentary procedure

Private Members' Bill procedure: an example of poor communication

Private Members' Bill (PMB) procedure is meant to give individual MPs the power to initiate new legislation. However, the procedure is complex and difficult to understand. The public are either unaware of the system and how it operates or find it opaque and inaccessible. MPs themselves find the procedures to be arcane.

PMBs can be raised through three procedures, the most important of which is the balloted bill. Each year a ballot is held at the start of the parliamentary session and the 20 MPs whose names come out top are allowed to introduce legislation on a subject of their choice. Members may also introduce Private Members' Bills in the form of Ten Minute Rule Bills or Presentation Bills. But these procedures are mostly used as a way of pointing out problems with existing bills or of raising issues to which the Government might not want to draw attention.

In contrast to Government proposals, few Private Members' Bills succeed in becoming law. In the 2003-2004 session of Parliament, only five out of the 38 bills that achieved Royal Assent were Private Members' Bills. The reasons why a PMB does not get through are also often shrouded in procedural subterfuge and in defiance of every genuinely democratic procedure, PMBs can be blocked by a single MP. The process inevitably raises unjustified hopes of legislative change, which are only followed by angry bafflement as a bill disappears down a procedural black hole.

4.75 Our principles affect not only Parliament's style but also its procedures. A thorough review of Parliament's procedures is as important as a review of its language. Some, such as Private Members' Bill procedure, is opaque to all but a few and frustrates a public with disappointed expectations. Parliament's job is on occasion technical, and there are activities which are genuinely hard to explain (dealing with amendments, for instance). But applying the principle of transparency to parliamentary procedure would have a significant impact. How are we going to get people interested in processes some of which are all but impossible to explain? Just as there has to be a wholesale review of parliamentary language, **we recommend that all parliamentary procedures should be comprehensively reassessed from the perspective of the communication principles we have advocated**.

4.76 Not only should procedures be as transparent as possible to the public. It should also be clear in respect of all proceedings what opportunities there are for participation, engagement and the inputting of views. As Parliament informs people of its business, it should also provide advice on how to take part. This might be sending issues or questions to a select committee in advance of their questioning a particular witness; or explaining how an issue-based discussion board on the parliamentary website will be used to inform Members on a standing committee when considering a relevant bill; or even providing opportunities for members of the public to make points or ask questions themselves at committee meetings.

4.77 Parliament also needs to be responsive to the world and topical in the issues it addresses if it is to convince the public of its relevance. Of course it must also act on those issues in which the public as yet show little interest, but are nevertheless of long-term importance. It is increasingly common for topics to be picked up and debated in the media and among ministers and voluntary organisations – but by the time Parliament finds an opportunity to discuss the issue the agenda has moved on.

4.78 Such topicality can be achieved by measures such as short regular debates and shorter notice for questions in the chamber. **We recommend that Parliament revisits and implements the recommendations on topical debates recently put forward both by the Hansard Society Commission on Parliamentary Scrutiny (the 'Newton Commission') and by the Liaison Committee.**[86]

A representative Parliament

4.79 The principle of diversity also has major implications for Parliament and how it comes across to the public. Despite improvements in recent years, our representative institution remains in fact hardly representative at all of the diversity of the country. This can only form a barrier to communication and engagement. A more diverse membership of both Houses and among parliamentary staff at all levels is another element in Parliament relating to, and communicating with, modern society. There should be better representation of women, of ethnic minorities and a greater range of ages. **The authorities in Parliament as they appoint staff, and the political parties as they select candidates, should recognise the need for such diversity if Parliament is to function well.**

---

[86] Hansard Society Commission on Parliamentary Scrutiny, *The Challenge for Parliament: Making Government Accountable* (Vacher Dod Publishing; London 2001) and House of Commons Liaison Committee, *Shifting the Balance: Select Committees and the Executive* (2000), HC 321

Examples of public participation:

The rise in use of **pre-legislative scrutiny** is seen as a move toward openness, participation and accountability in the parliamentary process. It provides a means to include the public in the early stages of the legislation.

Bills selected for pre-legislative scrutiny are referred to a relevant select committee or a temporary appointed committee. The committee can take evidence from external sources, explain why it supports or opposes a bill and recommend appropriate amendments.

Pre-legislative scrutiny can stimulate public and media debate on a subject. Pressure and lobby groups can campaign on the issue and may give evidence to the committee, to Parliament as a whole and to the media. Online consultations can take place. One recent successful example, on the Communications Bill, resulted in two of the Committee's key policy recommendations coming directly from suggestions made on the online forum. Generating debate in this way improves transparency and can increase levels of public participation.

Similarly, Parliament should explore the potential for **post-legislative scrutiny**, in which the impact and implementation of past legislation is reviewed at an agreed interval. Again, this procedure would provide relevant and effective ways to engage the public in Parliament's work.

In the case of pre- or post-legislative scrutiny far more transparent processes must evolve for selecting committees comprising MPs and Peers likely to offer a knowledgeable contribution to the process.

The **Scottish Parliament's petitions procedure** is another example of the capacity of parliamentary procedures to involve the public in Parliament's work and link communication from and with the public to other proceedings.

Any person or group may submit a petition to the Scottish Parliament. All petitions are initially considered by the Public Petitions Committee, who then make a decision on the action it considers appropriate. This typically involves referring the petition to the relevant committee of the Scottish Parliament or recommending that it be debated at a meeting of the Parliament.

A considerable number of petitions have prompted positive action, including the initiation of committee inquiries, legislative change and parliamentary debates. Outcomes have included, for example, a recommendation that a fast-track court should be created to speed up the compensation process for asbestosis victims and changes to legislation and guidance relating to land tenure.

The petitions system allows the public to raise issues of concern and was set up as part of the Scottish Parliament's commitment to openness and accountability. The Scottish Parliament believes it generates a feeling of participation in the legislative process and of being heard by elected representatives.

Accessibility is increased by the e-petitioner system, which allows a petition to be hosted on the Scottish Parliament's website for a period of time (usually 4-6 weeks). This enables the petition to reach a wider audience and gather more support. Petitions can also be good for the media and for increasing the space for public debate on political issues in general.

Our Recommendations

R8   A new Communications Department should set up an advisory group of media representatives

R9   Parliamentary officials should do much more to draw the media's attention explicitly to matters of public interest

R10 The rules of television coverage in the chambers should be relaxed to allow, for example, appropriate reaction shots, the relevant use of close-ups, more panning shots of the backbenches and a greater range of coverage during divisions. It should be an explicit objective of parliamentary coverage to not just inform but to interest and engage the viewer

R11 There should be a relaxation of the rules for filming in the precincts of Parliament, permission for walking shots, interviews with relevant persons other than MPs, and a wider interpretation of parliamentary subject-matter which genuinely reflects the richness of political activity taking place at any one time within Parliament

R12 The ban on still photographs should be reconsidered in light of the communication principles set out above

R13 The current restrictions on the number of passes available for media outlets should be reconsidered

R14 The parliamentary authorities should provide regular, formal induction for journalists

R15 A new Communications Department should establish effective processes to manage, edit, develop and continually update the parliamentary website

R16 The parliamentary website should be radically improved. At a minimum, it should be consultative, interactive and easily navigable

R17 An improved website should engage the widest range of citizens, using well-designed publicity and targeted advertising to help people understand that there is a virtual route through which they have easy access to their Parliament

R18 Parliament should consider its role in consistently developing citizenship education resources and the different curriculum approaches across the UK. It should work closely with other organisations to support more training for teachers, and more and better materials for young people

R19 Parliament's facilities, including the chambers, should be made available during recess for groups of young people

R20 Parliament should take young people, including pre-voting citizens, far more seriously by involving them in its processes and decision-making

R21 In line with recent joint recommendations from the Accommodation and Works Committee and Administration Committee, the Parliamentary Education Unit should have a well resourced and dedicated teaching space with multi-media facilities

R22 Parliament should employ more full-time and contracted staff who are fully trained and experienced in working with young people in a range of different settings

R23 A young persons' consultative group should be established with the right to attend and advise at key administrative meetings of both Houses

R24 More should be done to enhance the effectiveness of parliamentary outreach work

R25 There should be a thorough review of the language and terminology Parliament uses in accordance with our communication principles

R26 Parliament should hold more meetings outside London. Select committees, for example, should hold more formal proceedings and public events beyond Westminster

R27 All parliamentary procedures should be comprehensively re-assessed from the perspective of the communication principles we have advocated

R28 Parliament should revisit and implement the recommendations on topical debates put forward both by the Hansard Society Commission on Parliamentary Scrutiny (the 'Newton Commission') and by the Liaison Committee

R29 The authorities in Parliament as they appoint staff, and the political parties as they select candidates, should recognise the need for greater diversity if Parliament is to function well.

CHAPTER 5

MEDIA COVERAGE
OF PARLIAMENT

CHAPTER FIVE
Media coverage of Parliament

Much media coverage of Parliament, when it is covered at all, reveals the same pressures to report splits, sensation and personality, rather than explanation and information, as that of wider political reporting. This is not in the long-term interest either of Parliament or of the media themselves. The reforms to Parliament's communication outlined in this Report, if implemented, would provide a much-needed opportunity for the media to examine their parliamentary reporting and identify those parliamentary news stories which the public have a right to know and a desire to understand.

Public service broadcasting requirements will remain essential in ensuring appropriate coverage of Parliament. Such requirements must continue to apply to the commercial public service broadcasters and not just to the BBC. There is considerable potential to extend the variety of genres used to engage, interest and explain our key democratic institutions. As Charter Renewal approaches, the BBC should provide a clear vision of its role and ambitions for the reporting of Parliament over the next Charter period, and as part of that vision we would expect to see plans to significantly develop BBC Parliament.

5.1   In the introduction to this Report we set out the evidence for a decline in the amount of media coverage of Parliament. While new technology opens up ever greater possibilities for direct communication between Parliament and the public, conventional media reporting will, for the foreseeable future, remain the fundamental means by which citizens are able to be engaged with Parliament's work. To date, direct communication has tended to draw in activists: those who have taken the initiative to approach Parliament in the first place, or who are in networks which link up with political and parliamentary activity. But it is no less important that the less politically active majority are kept informed of what Parliament is doing, and are easily able to find out more once their interest is engaged. Television, radio and newspapers will remain for the foreseeable future essential media for the public to follow the activities of Parliament.

5.2   Government has adapted to the modern media world much more readily than Parliament. We have already identified some obvious barriers to the reporting of Parliament's work. These include the lack of a coherent and comprehensive

Copyright *The Times*

communication strategy delivered by a designated and effective department, outdated and unhelpful rules for filming both inside and outside the chamber, problems for journalists in covering Parliament and understanding its processes, and a seemingly unnecessary reluctance among parliamentary officials to highlight information of interest to the outside world.

5.3 Our evidence suggested that there is also much that the media can do to improve and develop their reporting of Parliament.

5.4 Many journalists currently reporting Parliament are at least as worried by the present state of affairs as MPs and outside observers. One went as far as to claim that if the legitimacy of Parliament was not bolstered through fair and sufficient reporting, the 'fabric of society and communities in which they operate and sell' would be threatened. Another complained that legislation was 'almost never explained' in the mainstream press; 'it is virtually impossible to find newspapers describing in any detail what a bill actually does.' We received many such complaints. The problem is primarily one of malfunction. There is no

We also heard criticism of media reporting of Parliament from members of the public:

'I think that the media are all too often part of the "Westminster club" mindset, i.e. they see themselves as insiders not speaking from the margins where the public are so often left. I also feel the media is still too London biased rather than any provincial outlook.' (Citizens' Panel)

'Successes are rarely reported whereas failures are commented on for weeks!' (Citizens' Panel)

'Both the media and Parliament are obsessed with their own individual "personalities". Where they "feed" each other, we end up with media men asking questions that are "wanted" and ministers doing some small favour in return. Sections of the British media are in terminal decline.' (Citizens' Panel)

'The politicians mock each other, the media mock the politicians therefore what possible opportunity is there for the general public to be informed or take any of it seriously …Those who have power (MPs, Parliament and the media) exercise it in a manner to exclude those who do not have any and only include on their terms. If we were to invent a democratic model from scratch what should/would it look like?' (Citizens' Panel)

'To me the media seems to focus on scandals, disagreements and arguments between the politicians. We know more about the personal life of an MP than the issues they are trying to put forward.' (HeadsUp Forum[87])

---

[87] HeadsUp Forum in evidence to the Commission. HeadsUp is an online debating platform for young people on political issues - www.headsup.org.uk

conspiracy of silence in Parliament, rather, an institutional failure of communication that needs to be addressed in a constructive way. We regard this as a key distinction.

5.5　When the Commission met journalists during a series of seminars in 2004, we heard concerns about the emergence of a media democracy, one in which it is difficult to oppose the media. It was recognised that political reporting tends to focus on the instantly packaged story and parliamentary debates often fail to provide this. Worryingly, we were also told that the lobby has increasingly developed a herd mentality, making it difficult for individual journalists who wish to cover alternative issues on any particular day.

5.6　There are specific public service broadcaster obligations placed on BBC1 and BBC2, ITV1, Channel 4, Channel Five, along with S4C, by the Communications Act 2003.[88] We shall discuss these later in this chapter. But in the case of newspapers, no such requirements apply. Indeed it was put to us that there was little point making recommendations to newspaper editors and journalists about parliamentary reporting. Andrew Sparrow from *The Daily Telegraph*, for example, ended a very helpful written submission by advising, 'I also know that newspapers do not respond well to being told what they should do by organisations like the Hansard Society, and so I think it would be unwise for the Commission to spend too much time coming up with recommendations on this subject.'[89]

5.7　From polling and our own evidence it is clear that the political and media establishments share low levels of public trust, that disengagement is taking place both from Westminster politics and from much media political coverage. Robin Cook MP has warned that, 'Viewers are literally switching off media stories of Westminster village gossip. The danger is that they will also switch off from democracy.'[90] Indeed, much of the public only read about their individual MPs in the local media. The Commission heard from representatives of the media that regional reporting informs communities by providing a local viewpoint on national issues. Local media regards itself as being outside the Westminster village bubble and tends to have better relations with their local MPs than is the case with the national media – as might be expected.

5.8　We do not accept the view that no one can usefully comment on the current culture of political reporting, that such proposals will be rejected out of hand by journalists and editors. The evidence we heard suggested that journalists

---

[88]　Communications Act 2003
[89]　Andrew Sparrow, *The Daily Telegraph*, in evidence to the Commission
[90]　Rt Hon Robin Cook MP, Hansard Society Annual Lecture 2002

are themselves eager to see Parliament given greater prominence in the media and would give a warm welcome to measures which helped them to report its activities in a fresh and engaging fashion.

5.9 Self-criticism and mutual criticism could be a powerful force for change in the media. As one former Editor of *The Financial Times*, Richard Lambert, acknowledged, there is currently 'very little peer group pressure in the print media'.[91] A member of the public told us, 'When a politician makes a mistake the media have a frenzy but vice-versa nobody questions it. It is essential to have freedom of speech in the media, but shouldn't the media be made answerable when incorrectly influencing public opinion?' While another thought, 'A bit more dog-eats-dog by the press would be useful too – but is there any sign of it happening?'[92]

5.10 Journalists have begun to discuss this among themselves. At a seminar in June 2004 newspaper journalists told us that the media must take some responsibility for coverage and journalists must be willing to correct themselves when necessary. In his study of power in Britain, the late Anthony Sampson acknowledged that many producers and editors were privately tormented by doubts about the deceptions and sleazy underside of their profession.[93] Peter Riddell commented at an award ceremony for political journalism that, 'The media should be far more merciless in admitting their own errors. Honesty need not be prim or sanctimonious ... It would be good if all papers had readers' editors or ombudsmen, not only as a channel of complaint, but also to write about readers' reactions. Moreover, we should also expose each other's faults [and] should no longer make excuses of the type "it may have been nasty but it was a good story".'[94]

5.11 We think that better communication from Parliament could play an important part in improving the quality of political reporting in this country's media. We call upon MPs to act in their own interests; conscientious political reporters to act in theirs; and the owners and editors to join both these groups in discovering whether a return to factual and fuller reporting of Britain's democracy might be of interest to her citizens.

5.12 **We believe that a radical reform of parliamentary communication and presentation provides an opportunity for the media to enhance their coverage of parliamentary business.**

---

[91] Richard Lambert, 'Socially Responsible Media'. Lecture for the International Centre for Corporate Social Responsibility, 1 December 2004
[92] Comments from member of the Commission's Citizens' Panel
[93] 'Anatomy of Britain' quoted in *The Guardian* 10 January 2005
[94] Taken from *The Times*, 2 July 2004

Public service broadcasters

5.13 The general Public Service Broadcasting (PSB) obligation on the BBC, Channels 3, 4, 5 and SC4 is, 'That those services (taken together) provide, to the extent that is appropriate for facilitating civic understanding and fair and well-informed debate on news and current affairs, a comprehensive and authoritative coverage of news and current affairs in, and in the different parts of, the United Kingdom and from around the world.'[95]

5.14 In addition the BBC has an obligation under its current Charter, that the Home Service, 'contain comprehensive, authoritative and impartial coverage of news and current affairs in the United Kingdom and throughout the world to support fair and informed debate at local, regional and national levels',[96] and that, 'The Corporation shall transmit an impartial account day by day prepared by professional reporters of the proceedings in both Houses of Parliament.'[97]

5.15 Ofcom has the responsibility to monitor the adherence of the broadcasters to their obligations under the Act. Ofcom has recently reviewed the public service broadcasting obligations and the BBC Charter is similarly now under review.[98] We welcome the reassertion by Ofcom of the importance of public service broadcasting and the emphasis on PSB as defined by purpose rather than genre of programming.

5.16 We are, however, concerned by some of the elements of the Ofcom review. In particular, **we believe there should be a renewed commitment by the commercial public service broadcasters to provide national and regional news and current affairs**. It is not enough to rely on the BBC. Engagement with politics, and with Parliament, will suffer if commercial broadcasters are allowed to walk away from such commitments.

5.17 Channel 4 argued that, 'There should be a specific responsibility to cover Parliament but the mode of coverage should not be narrowly defined. The BBC and Channel 4 clearly have responsibilities in this area and should

---

[95] Communications Act 2003 s.264(6)(c)

[96] Department of National Heritage, *Copy of the Agreement Dated the 25th Day of January 1996 Between Her Majesty's Secretary of State for National Heritage and the British Broadcasting Corporation*, (The Stationery Office; London, 1996), 3.2(c). Known as the 'BBC Agreement'

[97] Ibid., 3.3

[98] Department for Culture, Media and Sport, *Review of the BBC's Royal Charter: A strong BBC, independent of government*, (DCMS; London 2005). Ofcom's recent review of public service television was in three phases and included the following documents: Ofcom, *Ofcom Review of Public Service Television Broadcasting: Summary of Phase 1 consultation responses*, (Ofcom; London, 2004) and Ofcom, *Ofcom Review of Public Service Television: Phase 2 – Meeting the digital challenge*, (Ofcom; London 2004)

continue to do so.'[99] We agree. We have argued that Parliament is an essential component of our democratic constitution, that its daily activity should be communicated to citizens, that it does not have the resources of Government at its disposal to communicate its message and its work. Unless specific expectations from Ofcom are required of public service

broadcasters, and agreed through the Statements of Programme Policy to cover Parliament, such coverage can too easily become submerged beneath the welter of wider, and often Whitehall-spun, political news.

Left to right: Kierra Box, Matthew d'Ancona and David Puttnam

5.18 But such a specific requirement does not mean that coverage should be uncritical – and Parliament will still have continually to demonstrate that its activities have a claim on the attention of the public. Furthermore, any requirement to cover the institution of Parliament must serve as part of the wider test of facilitating civic understanding and fair and well-informed debate. Many who spoke to us felt there

was the potential for much more innovation and imagination in how the PSB remit was interpreted by broadcasters. The BBC felt that sometimes MPs were a brake on such innovation, interpreting every development as 'dumbing down'.

Left to right: Joe Hall, Fran Unsworth and Jackie Ashley

5.19 We would strongly support a more diverse approach to the PSB remit, extending its application to drama and other non-current affairs/news programming. There is a particular challenge in how PSB should reach those sections of society which are at the moment most detached from many of the political processes, for example young people and black and minority ethnic groups. Most young people do not pay much attention to mainstream news and so alternative 'entry points' need to be identified for them if their civic understanding is to be improved. Consideration should be given to an explicit requirement within PSB for the diversity of British society to be addressed, and the specific needs of young people met.

---

[99] Channel 4 in evidence to the Commission

5.20 Channel 4 told us, 'With regard to citizenship education, we are exploring the use of drama and narratives as means of engaging debate and awareness, and connecting the world of Westminster politics to the political and citizenship issues which are of direct concern to many young people ....'[100] We welcome this initiative and **we encourage all public service broadcasters to increase the quality and amount of political programming, particularly that designed to meet the needs of young people**.

5.21 The growth of broadband digital technology opens up the opportunity for truly local (as opposed to regional) television. While opposing any withdrawal from political and parliamentary coverage by ITV, there is no question that communication between local MPs and their electorate could be as well, or even better, facilitated by the development of genuinely locally-focused broadcasting.

5.22 The BBC has an obligation at present to provide a daily report on parliamentary proceedings.[101] With the extension of webcam access, Parliament's website provision and the daily production of *Hansard* on the web, a full record of proceedings is widely accessible. But programmes such as *Yesterday in Parliament* and *Today in Parliament* still provide for many an invaluable digest of the day's proceedings and we would not want such programmes to end. The BBC must, however, have a public service broadcasting obligation which takes the Corporation well beyond simply a daily account of proceedings in its reporting of Parliament.

5.23 In its own contribution to the debate over its future, *Building Public Value*, the BBC emphasises 'democratic value: supporting informed citizenship with trusted and impartial news and information'. It also identifies as a key component of public value the willingness 'to innovate and bear the risks that innovation brings'. The document reaffirms the BBC's commitment to serious news and prime time current affairs programming. Examples are given of the 'multiplier

Paula Carter, a communications adviser:
'The requirements placed upon the BBC to report Parliament and the perspective seen by viewers through news programmes do little more than reinforce the image of Parliament as a remote, introspective and adversarial club where men (and occasionally women) in suits try and outsmart each other. The workings of Parliament are not explained and the reporting of its activities is limited to political clashes simplified down to be digestible within a two minute news item.'[102]

---

[100] Ibid.
[101] BBC Agreement (1996)
[102] Paula Carter, communications adviser, in evidence to the Commission

effect' of BBC programming on society, such as work with the NHS on the subject of obesity. There is clear commitment to encouraging local civic engagement and to support devolved assemblies.[103]

5.24 This pre-Charter renewal commitment to democratic value in public service broadcasting is as welcome as it is heartening. The principles outlined above seem to herald absolutely the right environment for a fresh approach to the broadcasting of Parliament. All the more surprising and disappointing then to note the absence of Parliament from the document.

5.25 The failure to mention Parliament is not acceptable. **The BBC must be required by the Department for Culture, Media and Sport and by Parliament to be explicit as to how it plans to report Parliament in an engaging, innovative and accessible way as part of its contribution to 'democratic value'.** We believe the BBC needs to have an explicit commitment to explain Parliament to the public, both voters and young people, and engage them in its processes. This must be done not only through news and current affairs but also through other genres. The BBC should also be required to demonstrate innovation in this programming.

5.26 There is, for example, considerable potential for the BBC to engage with parliamentary consultations, be they for select committee inquiries or pre-legislative or post-legislative scrutiny of bills. Why, for example, do we seldom see Andrew Marr interviewing a Committee Chair when a key inquiry is announced, asking why the Committee is looking into the issue, what the key questions are and how the public can have their say?

BBC Parliament

5.27 The BBC has a dedicated parliamentary channel, BBC Parliament, and any consideration of the future of parliamentary communication has to consider how BBC Parliament can best be used to communicate parliamentary activity to the public. The channel has the occasional capacity to attract significant audiences and during an aspect of the tuition fee debate, for example, BBC Parliament had more viewers than either Sky News or BBC News 24. We believe that audiences could be expanded by increased cross trailing when relevant to news, current affairs and other programmes. Some of this is already routinely done, for example on News 24, but there is scope for considerably more. **We recommend that there be greater integration between BBC Parliament and the broader spectrum of BBC**

---

[103] BBC, *Building Public Value: Renewing the BBC for a digital world* (BBC; London 2004)

programming to improve cross trailing. The BBC told us that one reason why not much of this was done was the unpredictability of parliamentary proceedings as a result of the intrusion of statements and Private Notice Questions into scheduled business. For instance *Radio Times* listings of BBC Parliament, which began in February 2005, would be able to draw greater audiences to the channel if there were advance notice and a greater predictability of business.

5.28 The BBC is to extend BBC Parliament to broadband, which will result in three live streams rather than the current linear coverage of only one event. Broadband will also extend the number of viewers who will be able to access the channel. It will be possible to supply background information on parliamentarians and the subject of debate. We were told, however, that a lack of both resources and demand means not all proceedings of Parliament are televised. Only a minority of select committees are televised and none of the standing committees.

5.29 In considering the role of BBC Parliament we have to distinguish between two functions, one of which is appropriate to the BBC and the other not. There is on the one hand a parliamentary information service and on the other a broadcasting service. Parliament has moved over a short period to the webcasting of all public proceedings, a welcome advance. While there may still be improvements possible to the quality of such webcasts, the parliamentary authorities are to be congratulated on this extension to the accessibility of Parliament.

5.30 The BBC serves a different function – it is a broadcaster and has to take editorial decisions, selecting content and deciding on commentary. BBC Parliament's role is complementary to any more comprehensive 'service of record' provided by Parliament itself. The role of the television channel should be to attract as wide an audience as possible to the work of Parliament, and explain that work, both in the main chamber and in the committees. The new broadband service could be developed as an editorial tool. It has the potential to be used not just by students of Parliament but by the many individuals engaged on particular issues as a guide to current topical themes, e.g. climate change or binge drinking, to see how Parliament is approaching these questions at many different levels. There is also great potential to link up BBC Parliament with developing citizenship education programmes in schools. To this end, **given the availability of webcasting of all parliamentary proceedings, the remit of BBC Parliament should be broadened to permit the live coverage of other noteworthy parlia-**

mentary hearings or debates, such as select committee hearings or House of Lords debates, even when this clashes with a House of Commons sitting. It would be left to the BBC's editorial judgement which would be of greater interest to the viewing public. The result of the current requirement, to give one recent example, is that the channel was unable to follow the Anti-Terrorism Bill as it moved from the Commons to the Lords. This change is not designed to turn BBC Parliament into a general news or politics channel - the focus is still very much on Parliament.

5.31 Spending on BBC Parliament has remained relatively static at about £2.5 million per annum. The channel has a monthly reach of between 700,000 and 1 million people.[104] **We consider that the 'democratic value' principles contained in the BBC's own Charter Renewal document imply the need for a significant increase in resources to BBC Parliament. BBC Parliament remains a seriously undervalued democratic and broadcasting resource, with immense potential to provide innovative parliamentary programming. The BBC should, in the coming months, provide a clear and substantial action plan for its development, and for a targeted and ambitious increase in its impact.**

5.32 **We do not believe that resources for BBC Parliament should be at the expense of effective funding for high quality public service broadcasting on the main BBC channels. We recommend that the BBC should continue to provide parliamentary coverage across the full range of its output, where it has the power to reach mass audiences.**

Our recommendations

R30 A radical reform of parliamentary communication and presentation should provide an opportunity for the media to enhance their coverage of parliamentary business

R31 There should be a renewed commitment by the commercial public service broadcasters to provide national and regional news and current affairs

R32 We encourage all public service broadcasters to increase the quality and amount of political programming, particularly that designed to meet the needs of young people

---

[104] BBC in evidence to the Commission

R33 The BBC must be required by the Department for Culture, Media and Sport and by Parliament to be explicit as to how it plans to report Parliament in an engaging, innovative and accessible way as part of its contribution to 'democratic value'

R34 There should be greater integration between BBC Parliament and the broader spectrum of BBC programming to improve cross trailing

R35 Given the availability of webcasting of all parliamentary proceedings, the remit of BBC Parliament should be broadened to permit the live coverage of other noteworthy parliamentary hearings or debates

R36 The 'democratic value' principles contained in the BBC's own Charter Renewal document imply the need for a significant increase in resources to BBC Parliament. BBC Parliament remains a seriously undervalued democratic and broadcasting resource, with immense potential to provide innovative parliamentary programming. The BBC should, in the coming months, provide a clear and substantial action plan for its development, and for a targeted and ambitious increase in its impact

R37 Resources for BBC Parliament should not be at the expense of effective funding for high quality public service broadcasting on the main BBC channels. The BBC should continue to provide parliamentary coverage across the full range of its output, where it has the power to reach mass audiences.

CHAPTER 6

HOW PARLIAMENT RUNS ITSELF

CHAPTER SIX
How Parliament runs itself

The failings in Parliament's communication with the public stem from a system of administration which provides neither political nor managerial leadership. To establish a distinct identity for the Commons and communicate its work, the House of Commons Commission must be independent of the influence of the frontbenches and the whips. The administration of the House of Commons should be headed by a Chief Executive appointed to the post through open competition and separate from the departmental heads. Above all, MPs and Peers themselves have to recognise their obligations to the Parliament of which they are a part, stand up for its rights and value, and take full ownership of its management and direction.

6.1   In looking at Parliament's communication, wider issues inevitably emerge both about how Parliament fulfils its constitutional functions and how it administers itself. We acknowledge the recent efforts and real progress made by both parliamentarians and officials to communicate Parliament to the public. But these many and varied initiatives have proved inadequate in providing Parliament with a modern and effective system of communication. We have asked ourselves why Parliament has been left so far behind; our conclusion points to the need for some fundamental restructuring of the way in which Parliament administers its affairs.

6.2   Earlier we made the point that Parliament must communicate with the public as an independent institution, distinct from the Executive. In written evidence to the Commission, Hansard Society Scotland contrasted the independence of the Scottish Parliament with the dominance of the Executive over Parliament in the Westminster model. The failure of Parliament to assert its distinct identity must be related to the powerful influence that the Government exercises in the proceedings and administration of Parliament. This is not to deny that both this Government and previous ones have taken initiatives to reform and improve parliamentary life – the establishment of the Modernisation Committee is just one excellent example. But such welcome assistance cannot substitute for Parliament taking responsibility, as a mature institution, for its own affairs. For a communication strategy to be formulated and implemented there must first be clear political vision and direction from parliamentarians themselves.

6.3 It may be questioned whether there is an appetite among MPs to become involved in administrative matters. We do not believe that sufficient concerted and sustained efforts have to date been made to inform and involve Members in the communication decisions of the House. We also consider that the communcation agenda set out in this Report relates so centrally to the key activities of Parliament that in a short space of time a significant number of Members will be taking a sustained and active interest in this work.

6.4 The failings of parliamentary communication reflect structural weaknesses in parliamentary administration. In the House of Commons the administration is directed by the House of Commons Commission, established by the House of Commons (Administration) Act 1978. The Speaker chairs the Commission, the Leader of the House and Shadow Leader of the House (or a Member nominated by the Leader of the Opposition) are members, with three other members nominated by the whips for approval by the House.

6.5 There are a number of problems with this arrangement from the point of view of parliamentary independence and effectiveness. First, the Speaker chairs this administrative body although elected by Members principally with regard to how he or she will perform the role of chairing business in the chamber. It may well not always be the case that the person with all of the qualities to be an excellent Speaker of the House is at the same time the right person to manage the House's administration. Furthermore, the convention that precludes direct public criticism of the Speaker by Members, and that is understandable with reference to the Speaker's duties in the chamber, which require the confidence of the House, might also have the effect of deterring criticism of the way the Speaker chairs and directs the House of Commons Commission.

6.6 The statute also means that the House of Commons Commission, and thus the administration and communication policies of the House, are effectively in the hands of the Government/party frontbenches (and additionally, in the case of at least three Commission members, in the hands of people immensely busy with other responsibilities). **We believe Parliament will communicate its own messages confidently and effectively only when it is administered independently of frontbench influence. We therefore propose that legislation be enacted to provide for the House of Commons Commission to be elected by secret ballot, with members of each party voting for a proportionate number of Commission members from among their number.** We recommend this to the political parties for their consideration. We also believe the constitution of the House of Commons Commission should come within the remit of the forthcoming review of the Braithwaite Report arrangements.[105]

---

[105] House of Commons Commission, *Review of Management and Services* (1999), HC 745 - known as the 'Braithwaite Report'

6.7 That does not mean that we are in any way diminishing the Speaker's role. Given the importance of the office, the Speaker should still have an ex officio place on the Commission. Moreover, we believe there is a wider representative role that

Clive Soley, former Labour MP for Ealing, Acton and Shepherd's Bush (1997-2005) and Hammersmith (1979-97):

'Members do complain about the structure, and the most frequent complaint is that nobody understands how the management system of the House works. There is no clear perception of who is in charge of what.

'The problem is that the House retains a system of management that resembles an old-style local authority before the introduction of chief executives.

'Over the past day or two, I have asked more than 40 hon. Members from all parties to tell me whom they would turn to if they had a problem with the management of the House. The most important thing about the question was that, with one exception, nobody gave the right answer, given what the report recommends and says is happening already. More important, with the exception of the person who mentioned the regional Whip, everybody hesitated, paused and struggled to work out the answer.

'I was reminded by the [Braithwaite] report that the chief Clerk has been the chief executive for the past two or three years. I said to some people – I did not ask everyone – "If you were in any other organisation, whether it was public, private, a local authority or a hospital, whom would you contact?" Without hesitation, they answered, "the chief executive." But when I asked just a few whether they knew that there had been a chief executive here for two or three years, I received replies like, "You must be joking," and "I don't believe you."

'A hospital is in many ways similar to this place – because we have to respect the sensitivities of the staff, both doctors and management, but when we have doubts, we do not ask who is head of the oncology department, or who is in charge of the midwives – we write to the chief executive, who then takes the matter up.

'It was said that hospitals should not have chief executives because doctors should make clinical judgments. In this place, people say, "You can't have a chief executive because we are politicians and we have to relate to our constituents."

'However, the two are not incompatible. There could be a chief executive who deals with straightforward general control of management and who is accountable …On the other side, there would be the Clerks doing the things that they do so well. We should still need some domestic Committees, although we are all agreed – including the Braithwaite team – that there are too many of them.

'Sooner or later, we shall have to separate those tasks [of Chief Clerk and Chief Executive] – just as all other modern organisations, private or public, have had to do …The last thing I want to do is to produce such a work load for the Clerk's Department that the Clerks are unable to give time, attention and detail to their Committee and Floor of the House work. If they cannot do that work well, it will do enormous damage to this place.'

Taken from *Hansard*, Cols. 1068-1072; 20 January 2000

the Speaker is well placed to perform. Traditionally the Speaker has not undertaken media work around parliamentary matters but we believe in today's media age Parliament needs a human face, someone who can explain Parliament and be recognisably identified with parliamentary concerns. A number of Members could take on such a role but we believe the Speaker in particular could extend the scope and value of the office by engaging in such activity. The BBC suggested to us that, 'The level of ceremony surrounding the role of the Speaker might be examined. He or she rarely gives interviews or explains procedural issues in general, and yet is a repository of knowledge about Parliament from which the public might benefit.'[106]

6.8 It was argued during our inquiry that Parliament also needs the equivalent of a Chief Executive. The 1999 review of House of Commons administration, the Braithwaite Report, gave the Clerk of the House of Commons the additional role of Chief Executive.[107] While remaining a departmental head, she/he also chairs the Board of Management, consisting of the heads of the departments plus the Clerk of Committees. The problem with this arrangement is similar to that of the Speaker chairing the House of Commons Commission – someone appointed to their position for a quite different set of skills is expected to be able to run an increasingly complex administration. They might well be able to do so. But, then again, they might not.

6.9 We see no reason why the offices of Clerk and Chief Executive should be linked. It is vital that the Clerk remains free to give the Speaker and all Members direct and impartial procedural advice, but this office can be performed without being the accounting officer or answerable for the overall administration of the House. There should at least be the possibility of the House appointing someone other than the Clerk to such an important role.

6.10 The Braithwaite Report considered and rejected the arguments for an externally appointed Chief Executive. We have examined the reasoning of the Braithwaite Report but remain convinced that an office of Chief Executive distinct from the departmental heads, including the Clerk of the House, is necessary to recognise and drive through change consistently across all departments. We see no reason, with a Clerk of the House whose rights to give procedural and constitutional advice are protected, that a Chief Executive cannot be equally committed to the privileges and rights of Parliament, making them central to his or her administration and management of House affairs.

---

[106] BBC in evidence to the Commission
[107] Braithwaite Report (1999)

6.11 **We recommend that the administration of the House of Commons be headed by a Chief Executive, experienced in the management of complex organisations in the public realm, reporting directly to the House of Commons Commission.** A new Commission should be set up as soon as possible to undertake the review of the Braithwaite arrangements. Its remit must include the constitution and powers of the House of Commons Commission as well as the administrative organisation of the House of Commons. We trust, in assessing how the current system is working, it will look at communication performance. We urge the forthcoming review to support our recommendations of a House of Commons Commission chosen independently by MPs themselves and a Chief Executive. We refer this recommendation to the forthcoming review of the Braithwaite arrangements.

Our recommendations

R38 We believe Parliament will communicate its own messages confidently and effectively only when it is administered independently of frontbench influence. We therefore propose that legislation be enacted to provide for the House of Commons Commission to be elected by secret ballot, with members of each party voting for a proportionate number of Commission members from among their number

R39 We recommend that the administration of the House of Commons be headed by a Chief Executive, experienced in the management of complex organisations in the public realm, reporting directly to the House of Commons Commission.

CHAPTER 7

THE WAY FORWARD

CHAPTER SEVEN
The way forward

7.1 Piecemeal or incremental changes as a response to this Report would go against the fundamental conclusions of our work - that the administration of Parliament must be transformed, that the mindset of Parliament has to change to take into account the public's point of view and that communication has to be radically reorganised as a central democratic priority if Parliament is to function effectively. Incremental change alone would mean Parliament drifting ever further out of touch, with consequent damage to our democracy. A new Parliament has an opportunity to pause and consider what it is there for, and what the public has the right to expect of it.

7.2 Some of our recommendations require fundamental changes to the direction and administration of Parliament. But even while such changes are being considered, much can be done. Parliament can develop a communication strategy through the processes we recommend, the two Houses can agree appropriately increased budgets and the public can be invited in to explain to Parliament how they wish to be far more closely involved in its work.

7.3 We want to see a Parliament which is an accessible and readily understood institution, which people know how to approach, and when and where to make their voice heard, a Parliament which relates its work to the concerns of those in the outside world. This is the challenge.

APPENDICES

Appendix One
Commissioners

David Puttnam (Chair) worked as an independent film producer for 30 years. His many award winning films include *The Killing Fields*, *Chariots of Fire*, *Midnight Express*, *The Mission*, *Local Hero* and *The Memphis Belle*. He retired from film production in 1998 and now focuses on his work in education in support of which he has served on a variety of public bodies. In July 2002, David was appointed President of UNICEF UK. He received a CBE in 1983, was knighted in 1995 and was appointed to the House of Lords in 1997 as Lord Puttnam.

Jackie Ashley (Vice-chair) is a journalist and broadcaster on politics. She has 20 years' experience of political broadcasting, having worked on *Newsnight*, *Channel 4 News* and as a political correspondent for ITN. She was editor and presenter of *Their Lordships' House* – the first programme to use television pictures from Westminster, and then presenter of *The Parliament Programme*, when televising the Commons chamber was first allowed. She has also been Political Editor of the *New Statesman*. She is currently a columnist and interviewer for *The Guardian*, a presenter of *The Week in Westminster* on Radio 4 and *The Sunday Programme* on GMTV. She is also a columnist for *Public Finance*.

Patrick Barwise is Professor of Management and Marketing at London Business School, which he joined in 1976 having spent his early career with IBM. His many publications include books on *Television and its Audience*, *Strategic Decisions*, *Predictions: Media*, and most recently, *Simply Better*. In 2004, he led the independent review for DCMS of the BBC's digital TV channels. He is also the former deputy chairman of the Consumers' Association.

Stephen Coleman joined Oxford University in 2003 as Professor of e-democracy at the Oxford Internet Institute. He was previously director of the e-democracy programme at the Hansard Society and continues in the role of senior research associate. He has written and edited numerous articles and books on ICTs and public participation.

Matthew d'Ancona joined *The Times* in 1991 as a trainee, after working at the human rights magazine *Index on Censorship*. He rose through the ranks to become Assistant Editor in 1994. He is currently deputy editor of *The Sunday Telegraph*, which he moved to in 1996. He was Political Journalist of the Year at the 2004 British Press Awards. He is also a Millennium Commissioner.

Patricia Hodgson DBE began her career as a producer and journalist. She was Director of Policy and Planning at the BBC from 1993 – 2000 and Chief Executive of the Independent Television Commission from 2000 – 2004. She is Chair of the Higher Education Regulatory Review Group, a Governor of the Wellcome Trust, and a non-executive director of the Competition Commission and of GWR Group plc. She has been a Visiting Bye-Fellow of Newnham College, Cambridge, during the Lent and Easter terms 2004, and is a Member of the Statistics Commission and the Commission for Standards in Public Life.

Raji Hunjan was a teacher of English and media studies before joining the Hansard Society in 2000 as Director of Citizenship and Education. In 2003 she was appointed co-Director of Carnegie Young People Initiative, which promotes the participation of young people at all levels of democracy. She is the author of Parliament's workbooks for young people.

Andrew Lansley CBE MP was elected Conservative MP for South Cambridgeshire in 1997. From 1999 to 2001 he was Shadow Minister for the Cabinet Office and responsible for policy co-ordination in the Conservative Party. He was appointed Shadow Secretary of State for Health in 2004. Before entering Parliament, Andrew Lansley was Director of the Conservative Research Department and Deputy Director-General of the British Chamber of Commerce. From 1979 to 1987 he was a civil servant.

Martin Linton MP was elected Labour MP for Battersea in 1997. In 2003 he was made Parliamentary Private Secretary to Leader of the House Rt Hon. Peter Hain MP. Formerly a journalist with *The Guardian* and a Wandsworth councillor, Martin has written books on political funding, electoral reform and media influence.

Tim Renton was elected Conservative MP for Mid-Sussex in 1974. During his 23 years in the House of Commons he was Minister of State for Foreign and Commonwealth Office; Minister of State for Home Office; Government Chief Whip and Minster for Arts. In 1997 he was made Lord Renton of Mount Harry and now sits on the Conservative benches in the House of Lords. He has written three books, two of them novels and the most recent, a historical study of parliamentary whipping.

Peter Riddell is Chief Political Commentator for *The Times*. Prior to joining *The Times* as a political columnist in 1991, he was US Editor and Washington Bureau Chief at the *Financial Times* from 1989-91. He regularly appears on *The Week in Westminster*, *Talking Politics*, Radio 4 and TV. Recent publications include *Parliament under Blair* (2000) and *Hug Them Close: Blair, Clinton, Bush and the 'Special Relationship'* (2003).

John Sergeant joined the BBC as a radio reporter in 1970. He rose up the ranks to become the BBC's Chief Political Correspondent and Political Editor at ITN. Soon after his arrival at ITN in 2000 he was voted the Best Individual Television Contributor of the Year at the Voice of the Viewer and Listener Awards for 1999. He left ITN in 2003 to concentrate on writing and other broadcasting work following the success of his memoirs *Give Me Ten Seconds*. He also published *Maggie: Her Fatal Legacy* in 2005.

Richard Tait CBE joined the BBC in 1974, editing programmes including *Newsnight* and *The Money Programme*. He was Editor of *Channel 4 News* from 1987 until his appointment in 1995 to Editor-in-Chief at ITN. In 2003 he moved to Cardiff University as Professor of Journalism and Director of the Centre for Journalism Studies. He joined the BBC Board of Governors in 2004. He is vice-chair of the International Press Institute and sits on the Advisory Board of the International News Safety Institute. He was also a member of the Independent Review of Government Communications. In 2002 he received a CBE for his services to broadcasting.

Paul Tyler CBE was Liberal Democrat MP for North Cornwall from 1992-2005. After the 1997 election he was Chief Whip for the Liberal Democrats and Shadow Leader of the House. He served as a member of the Select Committee on Modernisation of the House of Commons from 1997-2005. Prior to entering Parliament, he worked for Shelter, managed a local newspaper group in the South West and, as a communications consultant, advised a variety of national environmental organisations.

Fran Unsworth began her BBC career in local radio and by 1990 she was producer and output editor of Radio 4's *The World at One* and *PM* news programmes. She spent several years as the BBC's Home News Editor before her appointment as the head of political programming at the BBC. In this post, Fran oversaw the corporation's review of political output following the 2001 election, leading to the launch of *The Daily Politics*, *This Week* and *The Politics Show*. Fran was recently appointed as the BBC's Head of Newsgathering, overseeing hundreds of journalists and producers in the corporation's bureaux around the world.

David Yelland is Senior Vice-Chair at Weber Shandwick. He began his career in journalism, joining the *Westminster Press* in 1985 and *The Sun* in 1990. He moved to *The New York Post* in 1993 and was quickly promoted to deputy editor. From 1998-2003 he was editor of *The Sun*, with a brief to make it the most important political paper in Britain.

Sian Kevill was also a member of the Commission between January and August 2004. We are very grateful for her contribution to our work.

Appendix Two
Terms of Reference

The Commission was set up to examine the communication of parliamentary democracy. It had the following terms of reference:

- To examine the presentation of Parliament and how that presentation is affected by the way it conducts its business

- To consider both the effect of Parliament's own procedures and the role of the media in explaining and publicising the work of both Houses

- To evaluate the potential for new channels of engagement

- To make recommendations for change.

Appendix Three
Written evidence submitted to the Commission

The Commission is very grateful for the written evidence it received following its request for submissions in April 2004. The information we received was detailed, considered and extensive and contributed significantly to our findings.

A full list of contributors can be found below:

Graham Allen MP

BBC

John Birch

Andy Birchall, *Chair, ON Demand Group*

Ron Bland

Damien Bove

British Youth Council

Paula Carter

Centre for Effective Dispute Resolution

Channel 4 Television

Daily Mail

Daycare Trust

Disability Rights Commission

Julia Drown MP

The Electoral Commission

Evening Standard

Lord Falconer of Thoroton, *Secretary of State and Lord Chancellor, Department for Constitutional Affairs*

Lord Feldman

Channel Five

Baroness Flather

Professor Bob Franklin

Douglas Fraser, *Sunday Herald*

Ivor Gaber, *Goldsmiths College*

The Guardian

C.E.T. Hall

Hansard Society

Hansard Society Scotland

Harriet Harman MP

Paul Hayter, *Clerk of the Parliaments*

Oliver Heald MP

Institute of Ideas

Institute of Public Relations

Nigel Jackson, *Bournemouth University*

Johnston Press

Michael Jolly

Kent Youth County Council

David Kerr, *National Foundation for Educational Research*

Robert Key MP, *Chair of the Information Committee*

David Lepper MP

Barbara Long, *Director of Parliamentary Broadcasting*

Melissa March

Helen S. McCall, *Carluke Gazette*

Des McConaghy

Medway Youth Parliament

Mary Morgan, *Director of Public Information for House of Lords*

MORI

Dr Ralph Negrine, *University of Leicester*

Richie Nimmo, *University of Manchester*

Liz Parratt, *Communications Adviser for House of Commons*

Lord Peyton

David Pollock

Michael Ryle

S4C

Roger Sands, *Clerk of the House of Commons*

Colin Seymour-Ure, *University of Kent*

Barry Sheffield

Joanne Simms, *The Oban Times*

Chris Smith MP

Andrew Sparrow, *Daily Telegraph*

Lord Phillips of Sudbury

Sutton Coldfield Grammar School for Girls

Viscount Tenby

Andrew Tyrie MP

Lord Vinson

Lord Wakeham

Perry Walker, *New Economics Foundation*

Tony Wright MP, *Chair of Public Administration Select Committee*

Baroness Platt of Writtle

Derek Wyatt MP

Young People's Working Group, Commission on Parliament in the Public Eye

Youth Action Kouncil, Staffordshire Youth Service

Appendix Four
Meetings of the Commission

The Commission held a wide range of meetings and seminars between January 2004 and April 2005. The full Commission met 11 times during this period and sub-groups of the Commission were arranged in addition to this.

The Commission was divided into the following sub-groups: parliamentary communications; media reporting of Parliament; public service broadcasting and citizenship; and parliamentary reform and modernisation.

The Commission and its sub-groups organised a series of seminars and events:

- **10 May 2004:** Seminar on citizenship
- **18 May 2004:** Seminar with parliamentary officials
- **25 May 2004:** Consultation event with young people and the Youth Voting Network
- **2 June 2004:** Seminar on public service broadcasting
- **28 June 2004:** Tour of Parliament
- **29 June 2004:** Seminar on newspaper reporting of Parliament
- **8 July 2004:** Seminar on parliamentary reform
- **19 July 2004:** Meeting with the BBC
- **14 October 2004:** Seminar on media reporting of Parliament
- **25 November 2004:** Visit to Scottish Parliament and seminars with parliamentary officials, MSPs and media representatives
- **1 February 2005:** Public meeting.

The contribution of participants at these events was invaluable to our work. Listed below are those individuals who attended meetings and seminars organised by the Commission and to whom we are very grateful.

Richard Allan MP

Steve Anderson, *ITV*

Paul Armitage, *Ofsted*

Phillip Atkinson, *Parliamentary Aide to Nanette Milne MSP*

Jillian Bailey, *Press and Publicity Officer (Select Committees), House of Lords*

Mark Ballard MSP, *Green Party*

Catherine Bebbington, *Communications Assistant, House of Commons*

Stephen Bermingham, *Commission for Children and Young People in Scotland*

Polly Billington, *BBC*

Members Only? Parliament in the Public Eye

Fiona Booth, *Hansard Society*

Malcolm Boughen, *Channel 4 News*

Gillian Bowditch, *The Scotsman*

Tony Breslin, *Citizenship Foundation*

Adele Brown, *Select Committee Media Officer, House of Commons*

Gordon Brown MP

Rob Burley, *Jonathan Dimbleby Show, ITV*

Dorothy Byrne, *Channel 4*

David Cameron MP

Jenni Campbell, *Outreach Services Manager, Scottish Parliament*

Brendan Carlin, *Yorkshire Post*

Paula Carter

Rob Clements, *House of Commons Library*

Alan Cochrane, *The Daily Telegraph*

Helen Collins, *European Parliament Office, Scotland*

Coombeshead College, Devon

Liz Craft, *Qualifications and Curriculum Authority*

Sir Bernard Crick

James Cronin, *BBC iCan*

Sean Curran, *BBC*

Mark Damazer, *BBC*

Lindsey Davey, *Events Co-ordinator, Scottish Parliament*

Carole Devon, *Director of Access and Information, Scottish Parliament*

John Dickie, *BBC*

Malcolm Dickson, *Holyrood Magazine*

Beccy Earnshaw, *The Electoral Commission*

John Edward, *European Parliament Office, Scotland*

Thomas Elias, *Private Secretary to Chair of Committees, House of Lords*

Erith School, Bexley

Esher Church of England High School

Rosemary Everett, *Head of Participation Services, Scottish Parliament*

Gerry Foley, *Tyne Tees TV*

Liz Foster, *Commission for Children and Young People in Scotland*

Douglas Fraser, *Sunday Herald*

Jessica Gold, *School Councils UK*

Tom Happold, *Guardian Unlimited*

Ginny Hill, *Jonathan Dimbleby Show, ITV*

Matthew Hill, *Department for Culture, Media and Sport*

Gaby Hinsliff, *The Guardian*

John Hipwood, *Wolverhampton Express and Star*

Greg Hurst, *The Times*

Robin Hutchinson, *Dod's Parliamentary Communications*

Kate Jenkins

Simon Jenkins

Jane Jones, *Participation Development Officer, Scottish Parliament*

David Jordan, *BBC*

Peter Kellner, *YouGov*

George Kerevan, *The Scotsman*

David Kerr, *National Foundation for Educational Research*

Phil Kirby, *Vodafone*

Kate Kirkpatrick, *Manchester University Students Union*

Peter Knowles, *BBC Parliament*

Jurgan Kroenig, *Die Zeit*

Victor Launert, *Central Tours Office, Parliament*

Barbara Long, *Director of Parliamentary Broadcasting*

Peter Lowe, *BSkyB*

Roger Lowry, *Ofcom*

Eric MacLeod, *Senior Media Relations Officer, Scottish Parliament*

Catherine MacLeod, *Glasgow Herald*

Simon Mares, *Central Television and Westcountry Television*

Jules Mason, *British Youth Council*

Sheena McDonald

Kate McGallen, *Department for Culture, Media and Sport*

David Millar

Mary Morgan, *Director of Public Information, House of Lords*

Gerry Murray, *Dod's Parliamentary Communications*

David Natzler, *Secretary to the House of Commons Commission*

Professor the Lord Norton of Louth

Liz Parratt, *Communications Adviser, House of Commons*

Peter Pattisson, *Deptford Green School*

Sir Robert Phillis, *Guardian Media Group*

John Pienaar, *BBC*

Keith Raffan MSP

Reading Girls School

Robert Rogers, *Former Secretary to the House of Commons Commission*

Alan Rusbridger, *The Guardian*

Dr Maggie Scammell, *LSE*

Janet Seaton, *Information Centre, Scottish Parliament*

David Seymour, *The Mirror*

Chris Shaw, *Five TV*

Joanne Simms, *The Oban Times*

Nicole Smith, *The Electoral Commission*

Stuart Stevenson MSP

Tim Suter, *Ofcom*

Caroline Thomson, *BBC*

Robert Thomson, *The Times*

Nick Toon, *ITV*

Alex Towers, *Ofcom*

Robert Twigger, *Parliamentary Education Unit*

Lucy Ward, *The Guardian*

Richard Ware, *Head of Office and Secretary to the Board of Management, House of Commons*

Chris Weeds, *Parliamentary Education Unit*

Paul Whelan, *Newsround, BBC*

Emma Wilson, *Vodafone*

Robert Wilson, *Principal Clerk of Select Committees, House of Commons*

Tony Wright MP

Sam Younger, *The Electoral Commission*

Appendix Five
Public Eye: Citizens' Panel

The Commission, together with the Hansard Society's e-Democracy programme, set up *Public Eye: Citizens' Panel* to look at how a panel of 'ordinary' citizens, in the form of a 'digital jury' could inform the work of the Commission. The 55 members of the digital jury were drawn from across the UK and were invited to give feedback on the weekly topic on the Public Eye website over a four-week period from 18 October 2004.

The project was designed with the view to encouraging people from all walks of life to take part in the panel. The Jurors were recruited through direct mailings, viral emails, web links and the BBC iCan website.

Members of the *Public Eye: Citizens' Panel* came together on the communal web site at www.hansardsociety.org.uk/publiceye to respond to a series of structured questions and themes for deliberation. The weekly topics were posted as follows:

- Parliamentary reform/modernisation

- Media reporting of Parliament

- Parliament's communication strategy

- Commentary in the media and miscellaneous

The site generated a lively debate, with over 350 messages posted to the site by panel members. These comments were summarised by the Hansard Society's e-Democracy programme and presented in a report to the Commission.

Appendix Six
Young People's Working Group

The Commission set up a Young People's Working Group with the support of Carnegie Young People Initiative. Kierra Box, Joe Hall, Christina Jessah and Roz Mascarenhas made up the four members of the group. Each has relevant experience and knowledge in the fields of politics, youth issues and media and all have been involved with youth organisations.

Over the lifetime of the Commission, the group reviewed evidence received by the Commission and held frequent meetings of its own. The group also participated in the following Commission events:

- Seminar on citizenship, May 2004
- Seminar with parliamentary officials, May 2004
- Event on young people, the media and politics, May 2004
- Seminar on public service broadcasting, June 2004
- Tour of Parliament, June 2004
- Commission meeting, June 2004
- Public event, February 2005

The group submitted its interim findings to the Commission in September 2004. As the Commission began to deliberate its conclusions, they identified the measures Parliament could take to have the greatest impact on engaging young people:

- Create an ambitious Communications Department with the remit to engage with the public, respond to their needs and seek out their interests – involving young people actively and meaningfully in all its review and planning procedures.

- Encourage and support MPs to give young people innovative ways to interact with Parliament which are relevant to them and where they can see real outcomes.

- Ease the restrictions on media access and reporting in Parliament (particularly television) and encourage them to report on the issues important to young people by highlighting interesting stories and giving them easily digestible summaries and searchable records of events in Parliament. Highlight to the media opportunities for young people to interact with Parliament or engage with issues Parliament addresses.

- Encourage young people to participate at all ages so they remain engaged later in life, from citizenship education beginning at an earlier age in schools to improved parliamentary websites which meet the needs of a range of young people.

The Commission benefited enormously from the ongoing participation and feedback from the group. The members enabled the incorporation of young people's views on an ongoing basis; these views have been included in the body of the Report.

Appendix Seven
Recommendations from other Reports

Some of our recommendations find support in earlier reports. Although by no means exhaustive, the list below gives an indication of assessments and recommendations that previous groups or committees have made:

House of Commons Select Committee on Modernisation of the House of Commons, *Connecting Parliament with the Public* (2004), HC 368

Too often the impression is given that the House of Commons is a private club, run for the benefit of its Members, where members of the public are tolerated only on sufferance. [2]

We are convinced of the need for a radical upgrade of the website at the earliest possible opportunity, which will require significant investment in systems and staff. The financial implications of this are for the Finance and Services Committee and the House of Commons Commission to consider. [11]

We recommend that, as development of the website progresses, the House authorities, in consultation with young people, develop the website in a form which is more accessible to them. [16]

We recommend that the Liaison Committee and Procedure Committee consider a process whereby public petitions should automatically stand referred to the relevant select committee. It would then be for the committee to decide whether or not to conduct an inquiry into the issues raised, or to take then into account in the context of a current or forthcoming inquiry. [29]

We believe that there is scope for greater co-ordination of the House's media and communications resources. We therefore recommend the establishment of a central press office for the House of Commons, to take a more pro-active role in promoting the House and its work. [31]

We recommend that the Board of Management and the House of Commons Commission urgently consider whether there is scope for further improving the co-ordination of the House's media, educational and communications resources and planning, with effective Member oversight and close liaison with appropriate officials and Members of the House of Lords. [32]

Members Only? Parliament in the Public Eye

Parliament First, an All Party Group of Members of Parliament, *Parliament's Last Chance* **(2003)**

It is vital that Select Committees are put under the control of backbenchers and not the executive or whips. We recommend that there should be division of chairmanships along party lines (as at present) but then the House as a whole should elect Select Committee Chairs by secret ballot. [p.9]

Parliament should reassert and re-establish its own identity and take more control of running its own affairs. At present the informal 'usual channels' systems tend to benefit the executive over the interests of backbenchers and the opposition. We recommend that there should be a Business Committee responsible for managing the parliamentary timetable. [pp. 13-14]

We recommend that a Petitions Committee should be established in the House of Commons to assess issues of public concern and if appropriate to make referrals for debate or committee inquiry. [p. 14]

There should be specific provision for 'public interest debate' or topical or urgent debates where a certain number of MPs (of all parties) request it. We recommend that the House reconsiders the merit of introducing a twice-weekly 30 minute session on a single topical subject. [p. 15]

To improve Parliament's communication with the public we recommend a well-resourced press office to publicise parliamentary activity.

We recommend that a Chief Executive should be appointed to run all Parliament's administrative and domestic functions. The Chief Executive should be responsible to a reformed House of Commons Commission which should be elected by MPs as a whole. [p. 16]

We recommend that Parliament should consider whether it is supported in the most effective way possible, whether the recruitment and working methods of its staff are compatible with the best modern practice and whether lessons should be learnt from the private sector and civil service, including more external recruitment, especially at senior levels. [p. 17]

There should be closer working arrangements between the staff of the two Houses. At present the two Houses work virtually in isolation from each other. Better channels of communication, improved liaison mechanisms and closer working between the Clerks, Libraries and other staff of both Houses would improve the effective functioning of both Houses and help develop a more coherent parliamentary ethos and approach. More practically, the absence of a combined and comprehensive management structure for the whole parliamentary estate causes duplication across a wide range of services and is very wasteful. [4.15 p. 56]

Commonwealth Parliamentary Association, *Parliament and the Media: Recommendations for an informed democracy* (2003)

Parliament should employ public relations officers to publicise their activities to the media which do not cover Parliament, and education staff to run outreach programmes to stimulate interest in parliamentary democracy. Both services should operate in an apolitical way under guidelines set by the House. [8.3]

House of Commons Select Committee on Information, *Digital Technology: Working for Parliament and the Public* (2002), HC 1065

The Committee recommends that the following set of principles for information and communication technologies be adopted for the House:

A. The House is committed to the use of ICT to increase its accessibility and to enable the public, exercising its right to use whatever medium is convenient, to communicate with Members and with Committees of the House.

B. The House is committed to using ICT to enhance the professionalism of Members, their staff and House staff in all aspects of parliamentary life.

C. The House is committed to the use of ICT to increase public participation in its work, enabling it to draw on the widest possible pool of experience, including particularly those who have traditionally been excluded from the political and parliamentary process.

D. The House recognises the value of openness and will use ICT to enable, as far as possible, the public to have access to its proceedings and papers.

E. The House will develop and share good practice in the use of ICT by other parliamentary and governmental bodies both within the United Kingdom and elsewhere, and will work in collaboration with outside bodies. [11]

The Committee recommends that the House report annually on its progress in implementing these principles. [12]

We recognise the importance of a communications strategy that maximises the accessibility and transparency of the House, and indeed Parliament. [13]

Regular investment may be needed to take account of developments in technology. [27]

Special efforts must be made by the House to engage younger people, who are recognised as being both more ready to use technology and more disconnected from the traditional political process. [50]

We suggest that the House Administration should: maintain an awareness of initiatives being developed elsewhere to increase public participation in, and communication with, representative bodies; work with others to use technologies in innovative and effective ways. [58]

Select Committee on Modernisation of the House of Commons, *Modernisation of the House of Commons: A Reform Programme, Second Report of Session 2001-02* **(2002), HC 1168**

We recommend that Select Committees and other parliamentary bodies step up their use of ICT to increase e-participation by the public in the parliamentary process.

The House of Commons belongs to the British people who elect it and who pay for it. [17]

We record our unanimous view that such an interpretative [visitor] centre should focus on the function of Parliament as a working institution at the heart of our representative democracy, and not just Westminster as an interesting building with a lot of history. [19]

Hansard Society Commission on Parliamentary Scrutiny, *The Challenge for Parliament: Making Government Accountable* **(2001)**

The House of Commons has been slow to adapt to the needs of the media. Whereas the Government machine, the political parties and most individual MPs, are attuned to the needs of the media, Parliament is not. To improve media coverage the Commons should sit earlier in the day and allow for morning statements from Ministers. [39]

Although both the Commons and the Lords have information officers both Houses need a designated press office. The press offices would be responsible for co-ordinating the press activity of the committees, highlight to journalists forthcoming issues and promote Parliament as an institution to the media. [42]

The House of Commons should re-establish a Petitions Committee which would play a significant role in mediating between issues of public concern and select committees. The committee should be structured along similar lines to the Scottish Parliament's committee and should draw the attention of MPs to issues where it feels there is public concern. [47]

The Commission to Strengthen Parliament, *Strengthening Parliament* (2000)

We want to build the link between citizens collectively and Parliament. We support the creation of a Petitions Committee.

We would like to see something of a culture shift in the attitude taken towards media access to the Palace. Parliament should be a far more open institution. [p. 24]

We want to strengthen the link between Parliament and the citizen. The best way to do this, we believe, is through ensuring greater media access to Westminster. [p. 54]

We favour major changes designed to ensure that citizens have a greater awareness of what Parliament is doing. There is some media coverage of Parliament and both Houses are pro-active to some degree in disseminating material about their work, not least through the internet. We want to see Parliament become an even more open institution. Citizens are entitled to see what is going on. Parliament itself benefits from the oxygen of publicity. It gives it greater leverage in its dealings with government. We want to see the media have greater access to the Palace of Westminster. [p. 56]

We recommend that the media be permitted to make greater use of the Palace of Westminster.

We think that camera crews should be permitted far greater access to parts of the Palace. Rather than stipulating those parts of the Palace to which the media are permitted, we think the onus should be reversed. We believe that camera crews should have access to all parts of the Palace other than those stipulated as off-limits.

We also recommend more dedicated facilities for the media within the Palace. We believe that there should be a room set aside for the media so that they will have their own technical support within the Palace and their own mini-studio. This would not only be for the convenience of the media and members, we also believe that it will provide an incentive for the media to devote more time and attention to Parliament. [p. 57]

House of Commons Commission, *Review of Services and Management* (1999), HC 745. Known as the Braithwaite Review.

Resourcing a Parliament effectively is an extremely difficult business. The House of Commons is no exception. The House has no mission statement; Members of Parliament have no job description. The Parliamentary process is to a great extent reactive, and the type and scale of activity is often dictated by external events. [2.1]

Yet the effective operation of the House is of enormous constitutional and public importance. The elector (and taxpayer) expects Governments to be held to account; constituents to be represented and their grievances pursued; and historic Parliamentary functions to be extended and adapted to changes in the wider world. [2.2]

These things do not come cheap, and no-one should expect them to. Seeking to hold to account a complex, sophisticated and powerful Executive; dealing with an unremitting burden of legislation; and meeting ever-increasing expectations on the part of constituents; all this requires substantial, high quality support. Add to this that the House of Commons is, in proportion to population, one of the largest elected Chambers in the world, and that its centre of operation is not a modern building but an inconvenient and expensive World Heritage Site, and you have some idea of the task. [2.3]

There is no shortage of complicating factors. Each Member of Parliament is an expert on what he or she wants from the system, and what the system should provide. With their staffs, Members are in effect 659 small businesses operating independently within one institutional framework. [2.4]

[T]he House and its Members are funded by the taxpayer. This spending is inevitably high-profile, exposed to media interest which is not always friendly and which may not pause to assess the wider value of Parliamentary expenditure. The House must be able to demonstrate proper stewardship of public money. [2.5]

It must also respond to changing expectations in the wider world…public bodies are now expected to be more transparent than ever before, to demonstrate best practice in governance and to be judged by the achievement of stated aims and objectives. [2.6]

We have noted that the Commission remains a shadowy body to many Members, and that it has not taken the more public profile recommended by Ibbs. We think that there is a balance to be struck. [15.12]

GLOSSARY

Glossary

Act (of Parliament): A Bill that has been approved by both Houses of Parliament and has been given the Royal Assent. An Act of Parliament becomes part of United Kingdom law.

Administration Committee: One of the domestic select committees of the House of Commons, advising the House of Commons Commission on certain administrative services for Members. Recent subjects considered by the Committee include access to the parliamentary estate and visitors during the summer months.

All-Party Group: Groups formed by MPs and Peers who share an interest in a particular subject, regardless of overall party affiliation.

Anti-Terror Bill 2005: Another name for the Prevention of Terrorism Bill, passed on 11 March 2005. The final passage of the bill necessitated over 30 hours of debate between the House of Commons and the House of Lords.

Backbench: Collective term for the members of parliamentary parties who do not hold ministerial or shadow ministerial office and sit on the Commons benches behind those who do hold office. Individually known as 'backbenchers'.

Blog: A shortened version of 'web-log', an online journal or forum maintained to express a writer's opinion on particular issues or events.

Broadcasting Committee: One of the domestic select committees of the House of Commons. The Broadcasting Committee advises the House of Commons Commission about the broadcasting of the proceedings of the Commons and its Committees.

Cabinet: The group of senior Government Ministers, appointed by the Prime Minister, who collectively decide on Government policy and co-ordinate the work of the different Government departments.

Central Tours Office: This office streamlines booking arrangements for tours of the Palace of Westminster and co-ordinates guiding arrangements and tour provision. In 2004, almost 112,000 visitors were conducted on tours organised through Members of both Houses.

Clerk of the House of Commons and Chief Executive: The senior official of the House of Commons, who acts as the chief adviser on House practice and procedure. The Clerk is also given the title of Chief Executive. The office of the Clerk of the House of Commons dates back to approximately 1315.

Clerk of the Parliaments: The senior official of the House of Lords, who acts as the chief adviser on House practice and procedure and also serves as the House's Chief Executive.

Commons Information Office: The office that provides the public with information on the work, history and membership of the House of the Commons.

Constituency: The group or area that an MP is elected to represent in Parliament.

e-Democracy: The use of electronic communications technologies to enhance and conduct democratic processes. The political use of web-logs, email mailing lists, internet forums and other online tools often fall under the collective heading of 'e-democracy'.

European Union: A supranational organisation of 25 European countries of which the United Kingdom is a member. The European Union (EU) gains its power over policy from areas that have been transferred to it by its member-states.

Frontbench: Collective term for the members of a parliamentary party who hold ministerial or shadow ministerial office and who sit on the frontbenches of the Commons chamber.

Government: The political party which holds the most seats in Parliament forms the Government of the day. The Government introduces the majority of laws considered by Parliament.

Group on Information for the Public (GIP): A cross-departmental group of senior Commons officials that aims to improve and co-ordinate public information and access. The House of Lords' Director of Public Information is also a member and Lords officials are involved in various sub-groups.

Hansard: The official transcript of Parliament which provides a daily record of proceedings. Hansard can now be read on the parliamentary website.

House of Commons Commission: Established by the House of Commons (Administration) Act 1978, the Commission acts as the overall supervisory body of the House of Commons and decides most matters of House policy. The

Commission is made up of the Speaker of the House of Commons, the Leader of the House of Commons, a Member of the House nominated by the Leader of the Opposition and three other MPs appointed by the House.

Leader of the House of Commons: The member of the Government who is responsible for organising the business (timetable) of the Commons.

Liaison Committee: The Liaison Committee is made up of select committee chairs. The Committee considers matters related to the work of all Commons select committees and advises the House of Commons Commission on select committees. It also chooses the committee reports that will be debated in the House and hears directly from the Prime Minister on public policy matters.

Member of Parliament (MP): An individual who is elected by the voters of a particular constituency or area to represent them in the House of Commons.

Minister: An MP or Peer who has been selected by the Prime Minister to have responsibility for a Government department. Opposition parties often select a 'shadow minister' to represent their party's views on the issues dealt with by the Minister and his or her department.

Modernisation Select Committee: One of the select committees of the House of Commons. The Select Committee on Modernisation of the House of Commons considers matters related to the modernisation of the House's practices and procedures.

National Assembly for Wales: The devolved assembly for Wales (Cynulliad Cenedlaethol Cymru) was created in 1999. The Assembly does not have the power to pass primary legislation, but can develop and administer policies.

Office of Communications (Ofcom): Created in 2003, Ofcom is the independent regulator and competition authority for communications industries in the UK.

Opposition: Political parties other than the Government party, whose role is to examine and question the work of the government of the day. The largest of the opposition parties is known as Her Majesty's Opposition.

Parliamentary Broadcasting Unit Ltd (PARBUL): The company, owned and operated by the major broadcasters (BBC, ITV, Channels 4 and 5, and British Sky Broadcasting), which provides to broadcasters the television images of the proceedings of the House of Commons, the House of Lords and of committees of each House.

Parliamentary Education Unit (PEU): The office that provides information and resources on the Houses of Parliament for teachers and young people.

Peer: An individual who possesses a title that either has been or can be inherited (hereditary peer) or is granted for the duration of the individual's lifetime (life peer). At present, all life peers and some hereditary peers are entitled to sit in the House of Lords.

Portcullis House: Constructed in 2001, Portcullis House contains public and private meeting rooms and office space for MPs.

Post-legislative Scrutiny: The term for an Act being reviewed by a select Committee after it has been introduced in Parliament.

Pre-legislative Scrutiny: The term for a Bill being considered in draft form. This allows Members who have some prior knowledge or speciality in the subject to consider the Bill before it is placed before Parliament.

Prime Minister's Questions (PMQs): The Prime Minister answers questions in the Commons chamber for half an hour every Wednesday. This is the most well-known part of the parliamentary calendar and a focus point for the media.

Private Members' Bill: A Bill put before Parliament by an individual MP rather than by the Government.

Private Notice Question (PNQ): A question in the House of Commons, for which no previous notice has been given, relating to a matter of public importance or the arrangement of business. Also known as an Urgent Question, it may be taken at the end of Question Time if it has been submitted to and approved by the Speaker.

Public Service Broadcasting (PSB): Electronic media outlets receive public funding to provide public service broadcasting. PSB arose from the notion that the function of broadcasting is not simply to satisfy commercial interests but also to inform, educate and entertain the public. For example, broadcasters are legally required to be impartial in their coverage of news and current affairs and must broadcast a certain proportion of current affairs during prime time.

Scottish Parliament: The devolved Scottish Parliament was established in 1999. As a devolved parliament, it has the power to pass laws on issues such as education, health and prisons, and to alter the rate of tax; other powers are dealt with by Parliament in Westminster.

Serjeant at Arms: The individual who is responsible for maintaining order and controlling access to the precincts of the House of Commons. The Serjeant at Arms is also in charge of housekeeping duties and the supply of stationery to the Commons. The office of Serjeant at Arms dates back to 1415 and the post has traditionally been held by an ex-serviceman.

Select Committee: A committee set up by either House to look at a particular subject area. Certain select committees examine the expenditure, administration and policy of each of the main Government Departments and associated public bodies, and also have the power to take evidence and issue reports on their findings.

Speaker of the House of Commons: An MP who has been elected to chair debates in the House of Commons. The Speaker's responsibilities include maintaining order in the House, ensuring that the Commons may carry out its business, and calling upon MPs to speak during debate. The Speaker ceases to be involved in party politics upon taking office.

Standing Committee: A committee set up by the House of Commons to consider the details of a particular Bill, and which only exists for the duration of the Bill being considered.

Standing Order: An order made by the House (Commons or Lords) for the regulation of its proceedings.

Westminster: The geographical location of the Houses of Parliament. The term is often used to refer to the body of political opinion formed by MPs and Peers, as well as those whose work centres on political matters (e.g. political journalists).

Westminster Hall: The oldest part of the Palace of Westminster, which includes a room that is often used as an additional and parallel forum for debate apart from the main House of Commons chamber. Following a trial from 1999 to 2002, the permanent Standing Order Number 10 was adopted to provide for the 'House sitting in Westminster Hall'.

Whip: An MP or a Peer who co-ordinates parliamentary business, and is responsible for maintaining party discipline to ensure that backbench members vote in support of the leadership.

Whipped vote: A vote held under close scrutiny by the whips to ensure that party members vote in accordance with the expressed party line.

Whitehall: The geographical location of many Civil Service departments and offices, often used as an all-encompassing term to refer to the Civil Service and UK bureaucracy as a whole.

Wiki: A website that allows its users to add and edit content, in contrast to traditional websites that can only be edited by those who have access to the site's HTML code.

SELECTED
BIBLIOGRAPHY

Selected Bibliography

Advisory Group on Citizenship, *Education for Citizenship and the Teaching of Democracy in Schools: the final report of the Advisory Group on Citizenship* (Qualifications and Curriculum Authority; London 1998)

Ashley, J., *I Spy Strangers: Improving access to Parliament* (Hansard Society; London 2000)

Barnett, S. & I. Gabor, *Westminster Tales: The Twenty-first-century crisis in political journalism* (Continuum; London 2001)

Baston, L. & K. Ritchie, *Turning Out or Turning Off?: An analysis of political disengagement and what can be done about it* (Electoral Reform Society; London 2004)

BBC, *Beyond the Soundbite: BBC Research into public disillusion with politics* (BBC; London 2002)

BBC, *Building Public Value: Renewing the BBC for a digital world* (BBC: London 2004)

BBC Governance Unit, *Governors' Genre Review: Current Affairs Television* (BBC; London 2005)

Brazier, A., *Issues in Law Making: Private Members' Bills* (Hansard Society; London 2003)

Brazier, A., *Issues in Law Making: Standing Committees* (Hansard Society; London 2003)

Brazier, A., *Issues in Law Making: Programming of Legislation* (Hansard Society; London 2004)

Brazier, A., *Issues in Law Making: Pre-Legislative Scrutiny* (Hansard Society; London 2004)

Brazier, A. (ed), *Parliament, Politics and Law Making* (Hansard Society; London 2004)

Broadcasting Policy Group, *Beyond the Charter: The BBC after 2006* (Broadcasting Policy Group; London 2004)

Coleman, S., J. Taylor and W. van de Donk (eds), *Parliament in the Age of the Internet*, (OUP and Hansard Society; Oxford 1999)

Coleman, S., *A Tale of Two House: The House of Commons, the Big Brother House and the people at home* (Hansard Society; London 2003)

Coleman, S., 'Connecting Parliament to the Public via the Internet: Two case studies of online consultations' in *Information, Communication & Society* Vol 7 No1 (March 2004) pp. 1-22

Commission to Strengthen Parliament, *Strengthening Parliament* (Conservative Party; London 2000)

Committee on Standards in Public Life, *Survey of public attitudes towards conduct in public life* (Committee on Standards in Public Life; London 2004)

Commonwealth Parliamentary Association, *Parliament and the Media: Recommendations for an informed democracy* (Commonwealth Parliamentary Association; London 2003)

Commonwealth parliamentary and media organisations and the World Bank Institute, *Parliament and the Media: Principles for an informed democracy* (Commonwealth Parliamentary Association; London 2002)

Cook, R., *Point of Departure* (Simon & Schuster; London 2003)

Cox, B., *Free For All? Public service television in the digital age* (Demos; London 2004)

Dalton, R.J., *Democratic Challenges, Democratic Choices: The Erosion of Political Support in Advanced Industrial Democracies* (OUP; Oxford 2004)

Department of National Heritage Broadcasting, *Copy of Royal Charter for the continuance of The British Broadcasting Corporation* (The Stationery Office; London 1996)

Department for Culture, Media and Sport, *Review of the BBC's Royal Charter: A strong BBC, independent of government* (DCMS; London 2005)

The Electoral Commission, *Voter Engagement and Young People*, (The Electoral Commission; London 2002)

The Electoral Commission, *Voter Engagement among black and minority ethnic communities* (The Electoral Commission; London 2002)

The Electoral Commission, *Gender and Political Participation* (The Electoral Commission; London 2004)

The Electoral Commission and the Hansard Society, *An Audit of Political Engagement* (The Electoral Commission and the Hansard Society; London 2004)

The Electoral Commission and the Hansard Society, *An Audit of Political Engagement 2* (The Electoral Commission and the Hansard Society; London 2005)

Erskine May, *Parliamentary Practice,* (23rd Edition) (Butterworths; London 2004)

European Opinion Research Group, *Standard Eurobarometer 61/Spring 2004: Public Opinion in the EU15* (Directorate General Press and Communications; 2004)

European Opinion Research Group, *Standard Eurobarometer 62/Autumn 2004: Public Opinion in the EU* (Directorate General Press and Communications; 2005)

Franklin, B., *Newszak and News Media,* (Arnold; London 1997)

Hansard Society, *None of the Above: Non-voters and the 2001 election* (Hansard Society; London 2001)

Hansard Society Commission on Parliamentary Scrutiny, *The Challenge for Parliament: Making Government Accountable,* (Vacher Dod Publishing; London 2001)

Hargreaves, I & J. Thomas, *New News, Old News: An ITC and BSC research publication,* (2002)

Home Office, *2003 Home Office Citizenship Survey: People, Families and Communities* (Home Office, Development and Research Directorate; London 2004)

House of Commons Accommodation and Works Committee and Administration Committee, *Visitor Facilities: Access to Parliament* (2004), HC 324

House of Commons Broadcasting Committee, *The Rules of Coverage* (2003), HC 786

House of Commons Commission, *Review of Management and Services* (1999), HC 745

House of Commons Information Committee, *Digital Technology: Working for Parliament and the Public. First Report of Session 2001-02* (2002), HC 1065

House of Commons Liaison Committee, *Shifting the Balance: Select Committees and the Executive* (2000), HC 321

Members Only? Parliament in the Public Eye

House of Commons Library Research Paper, *UK Election Statistics: 1918-2004* (2004), RP 04/061

House of Commons Library, *e-Democracy* (2004), SN/PC/2600

House of Commons Library, *House of Commons: providing information and access for the public* (2005), SN/PC/3359

House of Commons Select Committee on Modernisation of the House of Commons, *Modernisation of the House of Commons: A Reform Programme. Second Report of Session 2001-2002* (2002), HC 1168

House of Commons Select Committee on Modernisation of the House of Commons, *Connecting Parliament with the Public: First Report of Session 2003-04* (2004) HC368

Howland, L., *Logged Off? How ICT can connect young people and politics* (Demos; London 2002)

Kellner, P., 'Britain's Culture of Detachment' in *Parliamentary Affairs: Reflections on British Parliamentary Democracy* Vol 7 No 4 (Oxford University Press; Oxford 2004)

Lawson, N., *Dare more democracy* (Compass; London 2005)

Lloyd, J., *What the Media are Doing to Our Politics* (Constable; London 2004)

Maer, L. & M. Sandford, *Select Committees Under Scrutiny* (The Constitution Unit; London 2004)

Marshall, B. & B. Lloyd, *Making the case for politics: Paper prepared for the EPOP Conference* (The Electoral Commission; London 2004)

McKie, D., *Media Coverage of Parliament*, (Hansard Society; London 1999)

Milne, K., *Manufacturing Dissent: Single-issue protest, the public and the press*, (Demos; London 2005)

Milner, H., 'The Voters' Paradox: bringing back the knowledge dimension' (PSA Conference Paper; 2002)

Negrine, R., *Politics and the Mass Media in Britain* (2nd edition) (Routledge; London 1994)

Negrine, R., *The Communication of Politics* (SAGE Publications; London 1996)

Negrine, R., *Parliament and the Media: A Study of Britain, Germany and France* (Royal Institute of International Affairs; London 1998)

Norris, P., *A Virtuous Circle: Political Communications in Postindustrial Societies* (Cambridge University Press; Cambridge 2000)

Ofcom, *Ofcom Review of Public Service Television Broadcasting: Summary of Phase 1 consultation responses* (Ofcom; London 2004)

Ofcom, *Ofcom Review of Public Service Television: Phase 2 – Meeting the digital challenge* (Ofcom; London 2004)

Parliament First: an All-Party Group of Members of Parliament, *Parliament's Last Chance* (Parliament First; London 2003)

Phillis, B. et al., *An Independent Review of Government Communications* (Cabinet Office; London 2004)

Riddell, P., *Parliament Under Blair* (Politico's Publishing; London 2000)

Rogers, R. & R. Walters, *How Parliament Works* (5th edition), (Pearson Education; Edinburgh 2004)

Rush, R. & C. Ettinghausen, *Opening Up the Usual Channels* (Hansard Society; London 2002)

Russell, M., *Must Politics Disappoint? Fabian Ideas 614* (Fabian Society; London 2005)

Sampson, A., *Who Runs this Place?: The Anatomy of Britain in the 21st Century* (John Murray; 2005)

Save the Children, *On the Right Track: What matters to young people in the UK?* (Save the Children; London 2003)

Smith, G., *Democratic Innovations: A Report for POWER* (POWER; London 2005)

Stanyer, J., 'Politics and the Media: A Crisis of Trust?' in *Parliamentary Affairs* Vol 57 No 2 (2004) pp. 420-434

Tyrie, A., *Mr Blair's Poodle: An agenda for reviving the House of Commons* (Centre for Policy Studies; London 2000)

Tyrie, A., *Mr Blair's Poodle Goes to War: The House of Commons, Congress and Iraq* (Centre for Policy Studies; London 2004)

Walker, D. & N. Jones, *Invisible Political Actors: The press as agents of anti-politics* (New Politics Network; London 2004)

Wring, D., 'Politics and the Media: The Hutton Inquiry, the Public Relations State, and Crisis at the BBC' in *Parliamentary Affairs* Vol 58 No 2 (2005), pp. 380-93

Youth Voting Network, *A young person's agenda for democracy – one year on* (Youth Voting Network; London 2003)